To Ron Carter, a musician who is so critical and judgmental of his playing he reads music vertically as well as horizontally, and to all those other string instrument players who are equally *really dedicated* to the quality of their product and who know no limits when it comes to improving their knowledge, their technique, and their sound,

and

to the new school of luthiers who are not bogged down by old school dogma and whose imaginations are totally free to explore those areas of the world of sound which are still terra incognita—it is to these players and luthiers that I respectfully dedicate this book because their dedication to the exploration of sound is the product of love, without which nothing worthwhile or lasting is accomplished—

and especially to

June

String Instrument Setups

10 Setups That Will Make Your Instrument Louder, Better, and Easier to Play

By Chuck Traeger

Hal Leonard Books
An Imprint of Hal Leonard LLC

Published in 2017 by Hal Leonard Books
An Imprint of Hal Leonard LLC
7777 West Bluemound Road
Milwaukee, WI 53213

Trade Book Division Editorial Offices
33 Plymouth St., Montclair, NJ 07042

Printed in the United States of America

Book design by Kristina Rolander

Library of Congress Cataloging-in-Publication Data is available upon request.

ISBN: 978-1-4950-6499-9

www.halleonardbooks.com

Contents

Sevenword vii
Preface ix
Introduction xvii

PART 1 **Traeger's Principle and 10 Setup Adjustments**

1. Resonance Response Comparisons 3
2. Traeger's Principle 5
3. Setup No. 1—Endpins 9
   Exotic Wood Endpins—Three Nonslip Methods 13
4. Setup No. 2—The Sound Post 15
   The Sound Post—The Krazy Glue Effect 20
5. Setup No. 3—The Bridge 25
6. Setup No. 4—Teflon 29
7. Setup No. 5—Mode Matching 33
8. Setup No. 6—The Tailpiece 37
9. Setup No. 7—String Spacing 43
   Tuning in Fifths 46
10. Setup No. 8—The Saddle 47
11. Setup No. 9—The Fingerboard 51
12. Setup No. 10—
    Tuning Machines and C Extensions 55

PART 2 **Repair (Intcrnal) Adjustments**

13. Repair Adjustment No. 1—
    Decreasing the Size of the Neck Block 61
14. Repair Adjustment No. 2—
    Top Plate Regraduation 65
15. Repair Adjustment No. 3—Round Backs 71
16. Repair Adjustment No. 4—Flat Backs 73
17. Repair Adjustment No. 5—The Kay Plywood Bass 75
18. Repair Adjustment No. 6—Tuning the Bass Bar 79

PART 3 Ancillaria

19. The Mystery of Projection 83
20. Don't . . . 87
21. Motions of the Top 91
22. Useful Measurements for Bass 93
23. Troubleshooting 97
24. My Sound Post Setter 105
25. Repair Oddments 107
    Punch Hole in Rib 107
    Crack Alongside the Bass Bar 108
    Small Splinters Missing from the Edge of a Newly Removed Top 108
    Before Replacing a Top 109
    Finishing a Fingerboard 109
26. Bass Thoughts 111

Special Thanks 113

Sevenword

CHUCK TO THE RESCUE!

I've known Charles (Chuck) Traeger for more than thirty years. During that time, I have been very *un*successful in avoiding damage to my instrument.

Either I am not tall enough or the bass is not large enough, and someone or something always finds a way to bang into it. We're talking some serious damage here!

AAARRGGHHH!

Once the tears stop, I call Chuck and get right over to his place. Not only is he always a calming force, but he also carefully and patiently explains exactly what he can do to return the bass to its original condition, or perhaps even better. **These explanations often develop into a lecture on how science can benefit the setup and repair of the instrument, and they are free!**

Now, in clear and concise language, Chuck's new book tells bassists some of the things he does to make these miracles happen.

My hope is that repair persons will take some serious time to read his book . . . not just to benefit their own craft but also for the sake of the rewarding smiles of the bassists when they receive their newly repaired instruments.

Ron Carter

Preface

The purpose of this book is to explain how a string instrument actually functions when it is being played. Once this is fully understood, it is not difficult to show how the performance of this function can be improved by a series of adjustments, called setups, to individual parts of the instrument to enable them to vibrate more freely.

This book is intended to be an encyclopedia of all the adjustments, external and internal, that can be done to most string instruments to make them louder, better, and easier to play. The book didn't start out that way, so let me tell you how it got there.

On the cover, second picture from the left, is the picture of the top of a very special bass belonging to Ron Carter. It is special because it epitomizes the most skillful, forward-thinking workmanship possible that, without proper setup adjustments, produced only a sound that was choked and uneven. Several setup adjustments changed this sound to a thing of pure beauty. (For the story of this bass, read the following introduction.) That is what this book is all about—how the sound of the most critical building and repair in all string instruments with a movable bridge and movable (as opposed to rigid) tailpiece, or one that can be made movable, can be immensely improved with proper setup.

The first picture, taken quite recently, is of an Ibanez electric guitar, which I worked on. The owner never played it because the sound was dead. The third corollary to Traeger's Principle states, "Anything done to any part of the instrument that makes it easier for that part to vibrate more freely will have a positive effect on the sound and playability." So, I removed the fixed rigid metal tailpiece and replaced it with an ebony movable one. The volume, the quality of the sound, and the playability of the instrument immediately improved noticeably. Before I had done this job, the corollary was merely a prediction. The success of this work proved the strength and validity of Traeger's Principle and proved to be the finishing touch to the book.

The two pictures are there because they represent the alpha and the omega of the discoveries and knowledge in this book: both instruments profited from setup adjustments proposed by Traeger's Principle. This is a rule governing the behavior of string instruments with a movable bridge and a movable tailpiece, or one that can be made movable. If you have such an instrument and would like it to be louder, better, and easier to play, read on.

If you are a bass player with a computer you probably have a pretty good idea of what and who I am, but if you play another instrument, let me give you a short résumé of myself. I was a successful bass player in New York City. I started playing in mainstream jazz ensembles, making my first record in 1945 and continuing to record for another ten years. I made records with Bunk Johnson, Sidney Bechet, Wild Bill Davison, Pee Wee Erwin, and others. Later on I played in the show bands of the Waldorf-Astoria and the Plaza hotels. I opened up my first repair shop in 1969 as a luthier specializing in the bass. For the purpose of empirical research into string instrument sound, this was a very fortunate happenstance, as I will explain shortly.

In 1971 I started what would become a lifelong friendship with Carleen Hutchins. She was one of the leading scientific researchers in the field of string instruments acoustics. Early on she said that if I did anything that changed the sound of the instrument, it would happen more in a bass than any other instrument. She was right.

In 1959 I received a BS degree in civil engineering from Columbia School of Engineering. So, when I studied the bass, I did not look on it as some mysterious work of art, but as a man-made structure obeying all the laws of physics and engineering that any other man-made structure did. But when I listened to the sound of the instrument I was working on, I listened with the professional ears of a trained successful musician.

Over the years I made several discoveries of adjustments that would make the bass sound better and easier to play. But they were in different parts of the bass. One discovery was in the endpin and another was in the nut—at the opposite end of the bass.

As I made more discoveries, I began to realize they were all related to one another and not disparate items. It was from this realization that I started to formulate Traeger's Principle for bass. As the principle expanded to cover other instruments, I rewrote it appropriately.

It is my belief that before I wrote this book that to most people, it didn't matter how thick or how thin or how wide a neck/fingerboard was, as long as it was easy for the hand and the fingers. It didn't matter how poorly or how well a nut or a saddle was made because they were just "instrument furniture." It didn't matter how the neck was attached to the body, as long as it was solid. It didn't matter how big or how small or how heavy or how light a tailpiece was because it was just "furniture." If you had a badly damaged rib, it didn't matter if you doubled the rib instead of repairing each crack separately because the rib was there only to hold the top and back together. The ends of the sound post had to be fitted to the curve of the top and back as well as possible because that was the way it had always been done. I could go on, but you get the idea. **This book will put an end to all that because they *all* matter to the sound of the instrument!**

To reach what I call Optimum Sound you have to make as many different parts of the instrument as you can vibrate as freely as possible, because they are all connected.

It was through a very circuitous route that I finally came to talk to John Cerullo, group publisher at Hal Leonard Performing Arts Publishing Group, about this book. One of the very first questions he asked was whether my discoveries could be used in other instruments. I immediately realized they could, because I recalled Carleen Hutchins's relating to me how she improved the sound of a viola by taping a penny to the tailpiece—a form of mode matching described later in this book. Then I remembered how a colleague, Gary Rickman, had improved the sound of a mandolin by doing one of the setup adjustments I had written about in another book.

The third corollary of Traeger's Principle states that if you can make any single part of an instrument vibrate more freely, doing so will have a positive impact on the sound and playability of the instrument. When I wrote that, it was just a prediction based on my experience. I discovered a guitar player with a guitar he didn't play because the sound was dead. He graciously loaned it to me. I removed the fixed, rigid metal tailpiece and replaced it with an ebony one, which was free to vibrate. I was thrilled with the positive result of the experiment. It validated Traeger's Principle for me, once and for all, at the same time that it expanded the reach of the principle. And that is why the picture of the guitar is on the book cover. Writing about it is a fitting finish to this book.

The dictionary definition of a *principle* is: "That from which anything proceeds." I now know that my principle can be applied to *any* string instrument with a movable bridge and a movable (as opposed to rigid) tailpiece, or one that can be made movable.

It was about this time that I pondered whether I should rewrite the book from a one-size-fits-all (or almost all) string instrument perspective, or to continue as a book from a bass specialist's viewpoint. I realized that the bass had more opportunities for optimizing adjustments than any other instrument. For example, you can't do an endpin adjustment to a violin. Going further, you can't do a sound post adjustment to a mandolin. But there are other setup adjustments you can do to both instruments that will improve things noticeably.

I don't think I would have made as many discoveries on a small instrument as I did on the bass, in which case this book might never have been written. So, what I have done is write a book about the bass and its many opportunities for improvement in sound and playability. Then, at the head of each different setup chapter I have written a short note telling you exactly which instrument or instruments that particular setup adjustment will benefit. If you play an instrument other than the bass, when you come to the word *bass* in the book, just substitute the word for your instrument in its place and all will be fine.

If you asked twelve real estate brokers what was the *most* important part of their business for clients and customers alike, they would all give you one answer: location, location, location! If you asked twelve bass luthiers the same question, I am sure you would get more than one answer. In fact, I am sure you would get several. And if a few of them agreed, it would probably be on good repair.

If you asked me, I would answer without hesitation: setup, setup, setup! for two good reasons. No.1: Even the worst instrument can benefit from proper external setup adjustments. No. 2: Even the best instrument can benefit from proper external setup adjustments. And for those luthiers who say good repair is more important, I have this answer: What good is the most thoughtful, carefully executed repair if the instrument still sounds like a Garcia Grande cigar box with strings because of poor setup, or none at all? (I recently had in my shop a prime example of this type of problem. In the following introduction I will relate how a certain bass came to my shop and how it left, because the story is not only interesting, it is also instructive.) Later in the book I will discuss what I call repair (internal) adjustments, because they can be done only with the top off. In part 2, I have tried to make this book an encyclopedia of all the now known adjustments, both external and internal, that benefit the entire string family of instruments.

The overwhelming and singular importance of proper setup is the subject and primary reason for my writing this book. I will give you ten simple setups to individual parts of the instrument that will improve the sound and playability of your instrument immediately and noticeably.

Before we go any further, I want to make something abundantly clear—everything you read in this book is true. It is real. It is an actual fact that you can hold in your hand and hear with your ear. There is no guesswork here, and no old-school outdated dogma.

I have been trying for years in my shop, in my writings, and now with this book, to show that modern scientific research can contribute a great deal of beneficial information to the setup and repair of string instruments.

Getting this word out, however, has been harder than I imagined. I expected resistance from well-established luthiers who have a successful career doing what others before them have been doing for centuries. Why should they change? And I have been getting some resistance from players who are either skeptical or who don't understand what I am trying to do.

Let me start by explaining that there are three enemies of sound. The first two are immediately recognizable because, like soldiers in an army, they wear a uniform that is easily recognizable. It is the uniform of too much—too much mass and too much rigidity. Too much mass is generally caused by wood that is too thick. This is almost always the result of repairs made with wood that is too thick, or sometimes due to faulty initial construction. Too much rigidity is generally the result of too much mass. Although, sometimes too much rigidity is caused by the wrong choice of wood for the job, such as repair cleats made from maple. That is why, for example, nobody ever makes a sound post out of ebony. Either way, these two enemies stand in the way of proper vibration and good sound.

The third enemy is much more elusive because he is a fifth columnist, a saboteur who hides, unbeknownst to his host, from players and luthiers alike. He is called ignorance. Don't get me wrong. I am not calling anyone stupid. There is a difference between ignorance and stupidity. Stupidity can't be fixed. Fortunately, there is a cure for ignorance. The cure is called knowledge—knowledge of facts. The dictionary definition of *fact* is, "That which has actual existence . . ."

When I opened my first shop, after almost a year, I put up a sign at the end of my work bench that read, "Before your instrument leaves this shop we BOTH must be satisfied." The reason I did this was because a lot of my customers were ready to accept so much less in sound than could be gotten out of their instruments. They did this because they were ignorant of what could actually be accomplished. This was not their fault. That wasn't their business. It was mine. Their business was playing. Fortunately, my jazz players, who were equally ignorant, always kept asking for more, hoping I could oblige. It is from them that I kept learning.

This book is full of facts—I want to replace ignorance with knowledge! All you have to do is read my books, think about what you have read, and try out the ideas. When you find that what I have written actually works, you will have knowledge of a fact. You will be free of guesswork forever because you will know.

In the world of bass specialists I find it hard to believe that there are not some who know a little bit about how to make the bass sound better. But as Alexander Pope said in a poem entitled "Essay on Man": "A little knowledge is a dangerous thing. Drink deep, or taste not the Pierian Spring." The reason a little knowledge is dangerous is that it may lull you into thinking you know more than you really do. With forty years of acoustic research I have tried to drink as deeply as possible.

There were two events which got me thinking about a book like this. In 2011 I wrote a post on TALKBASS. In response to my post I received over six pages of replies. I skipped the nerdy ones, read with gratification the positive ones, and read the negative ones with interest because some of them were well-thought-out, constructive criticisms. But the most important thing I learned was that I was failing to reach a great many of my readers with my message. That was my fault, not theirs.

I will give you some examples of the replies. One respondent suggested that people should take my principle with a grain of salt. The person writing that had absolutely no idea of what I was trying to do because of my failure to communicate. Another—a luthier, I suspect—said he would rather trust his own intuition. This is the type of resistance I had been anticipating.

This latter is the result of old-school dogma that has had a stranglehold on people's thinking for a long, long time. People are reluctant to abandon a long-held comfortable way of thinking. It has been this way ever since Galileo declared that the world circled the sun, and not the other way around.

Why these people were not curious enough to try a few of my suggestions before they wrote is entirely beyond me. In my opinion, lack of curiosity is a major impediment to progress.

For these two people, and others of like mind, I have this to say—please, *please* read what I have written in this book about sound posts. Then do it. It won't take much time and certainly not much effort. Then listen. If this does not convince you of the truth and efficacy of Traeger's Principle, something is wrong.

In my first book, *The Setup and Repair of the Double Bass for Optimum Sound*, I was trying to make people think in a different way, to show that modern science has a great deal to offer the present and future crop of luthiers.

However, there was one comment in particular that I cherish. It was about a bass that had an annoying "halo" of sound around the basic note. (Thank you, Chris Fitzgerald, for that perfect descriptive word.) I realized immediately that I had not included this phenomenon in my principle. I have rectified this omission in chapter 2.

When I wrote that first book, I put them side by side. As a result, what I knew of setup (I know more now) became buried under repair. Even the poorest instrument can benefit from proper setup. With this book I want to show how important proper setup is to Optimum Sound.

The second event was a rather discouraging realization. I know three repairers who had read my books. Of the three of them only one remembered anything at all. He remembered a couple of things, one of which intrigued him because he was already interested in the subject. If they don't read to learn and remember, how can they start to improve what they are doing?

I thought about this problem, and tried to figure out a way to make remembering easier. I finally realized that if I put each setup idea in a separate chapter and in a separate book, the ideas would be easier to think about and assimilate. At least this is my hope.

I have come to understand that it has been hard for people to translate the abstract words of Traeger's Principle into concrete, workable reality. So, at the head of each chapter in this book I will be stating that part or parts of the principle that apply to the subject.

These setups will not give the same amount of improvement on different instruments. The closer the instrument already is to Optimum Sound, the less the improvement, and vice versa. On a scale of 1 to 10, some will give you 10 plus, others only 1 or 2, but all are positive improvements; put them all together, they will make you (and your instrument) very happy.

Student-grade instruments will probably give you the greatest amount of improvement. They are not great instruments, but they are a fair enough grade to respond well to the setup adjustments recommended in this book. Since they have more room for improvement than much finer instruments, the improvement will be more noticeable.

This book is not to be read and put aside. This book is to be read and reread and studied until the reader has a full understanding of what I have written. I am convinced that the great majority of instruments have been asleep since they were built. It is time to wake them up with these setup adjustments and let them play to their full potential!

If you play other instruments, read each setup carefully, then try it on your particular instrument.

Introduction

Of all the knowledge that a good luthier can possess, the knowledge of proper setup is far and away the most important. Why? Because proper setup can change a clunker into a good workman bass (or instrument); proper setup can make a very good bass into a superb world-class instrument. The most exquisite repair done by a fastidious luthier cannot do that. All it can do is make an excellent foundation for proper setup. This book is designed to be an encyclopedia of all the latest knowledge of all the things that can make a bass sound better and easier to play.

It wasn't until June 2012 that I truly understood the supreme importance of proper setup to the sound of the bass. It was an event in my shop which prompted this book.

I had heard of a luthier named Gary Rickman, who had rediscovered an antique method of making tops that was discarded long ago because it was so time consuming as to be uneconomical.

A friend of his, who was a bass player, persuaded him to make a top in this manner for a bass. The finished instrument turned out so well that the owner is now playing it exclusively in preference to his $20,000 bass. I talked to him and listened as he raved about his new top. So, I took a chance, called Ron Carter, and recommended that he send him a bass to work on.

Gary is a violin maker by trade and a bass specialist by popular demand. His violins are very loud, very responsive, and project well. They are also egregiously underpriced at $7,000 apiece. My advice is to buy his violins now because in a few years, when more famous players start using them, the price will skyrocket. Itzhak Perlman would do well to buy some for his best students, as they will be played for a long time.

Several years previously Marvin Topolsky, then a player in the Metropolitan Opera Orchestra, had sent me a bass for repair and subsequent sale. When I had finished the repair, I was so impressed with the sound that I called Ron and told him he should listen to this bass. He did and immediately purchased the instrument. But the bass had some playing problems. The fingerboard had a rather deep curve to accommodate gut strings, and the stand height (the distance between the underside of the fingerboard at the neck butt and the top of the bass) was only about

(Violin and photo
by Gary Rickman.)

½ inch (13 mm), making playing in the upper register difficult. This was the bass he sent to Gary.

Gary not only made a new top for the agreed-upon price, but went further and redid the fingerboard curve and reset the neck at a proper stand height, necessitating a new taller bridge. He then varnished the new top to correspond exactly to the color of the rest of the bass. The workmanship on everything was superb.

Gary had driven all the way from Chicago to bring the bass to my house so I could see and hear it. My friend (and excellent bassist) Robert Kopec hadn't played more than four notes when I was astonished. The sound was not at all what I had expected from a masterwork of the luthier's art in both building and repairing. Both Robert and I agreed. It was choked, uncentered sounding, and unfocused. Robert complained that the sound was uneven across the strings in the upper register.

The problem was not in Gary's workmanship, which was superb. What had happened was that he did not know how important proper setup was to improving the sound of the bass. Many contemporary luthiers are unaware of how important this is. Lack of knowledge is neither a crime nor a negative reflection on a person's character. The paramount reason for this book is to correct that situation by spreading this knowledge.

So, I sat down and studied the bass. I could see several areas where I knew I could make setup changes that would improve the sound. The first thing I did was to remove the sound post and round the edges of both ends like the player's end of a drumstick. When the post was inserted, the sound immediately became louder and a bit more focused. The next thing I did was to check the mode match of the neck fingerboard against that of the tailpiece.

The neck/fingerboard tap-tone note was a C. That of the tailpiece was an E. I knew from experience that a major third was the maximum difference in tones that could be matched. Because the lower bout was quite a bit shorter in distance from the bridge to the saddle, the top's maker had wisely chosen a half-size tailpiece. We extended the tailpiece hanger cable until we finally got a mode match. But now the tailpiece was so close to the bridge that the E string sound had died. Fortunately, I had a quarter-size tailpiece in stock. We replaced the half-size tailpiece with the quarter-size, adjusted the cable hanger wire length until we had a match, and the tailpiece was now far enough away from the bridge that the E string was no longer muted. Furthermore, the unevenness across the strings in the upper register had disappeared and the sound was louder.

But now we had another problem. Because the tailpiece was so light, the sound was too bright, almost tinny. We cut some pieces of 0.008-inch-thick Teflon fabric and inserted them between the bridge feet and the bass top. The sound immediately became warmer and more open.

But with all this work we had to detune and retune the bass many times. Each time I touched the tuning fork to the top so that we could tune it up, the bass never rang back. My test for a perfectly setup bass is to hear the top continue to ring after the tuning fork has been removed. I guessed that the sound post was too tight. We removed it, shortened it a bit, and replaced it. This time when I touched the tuning fork to the top and then removed it, the top kept on ringing a loud A note. The bass sound was completely free, no longer choked and unfocused. A top is freer to vibrate properly and produce a better sound with a sound post that is seemingly too short to most bass luthiers. (I have Bill Merchant to thank for this discovery. He fits his posts so they just slide in, with almost no top deflection at all, with the D and G strings off the bridge and the E and A on the bridge, tuned down a fourth.) Remove the slight pressure of the E and A strings and the post will probably topple over.

I was ecstatic. The sound had changed. It was like a beautiful piece of Lalique glass, pure and crystal clear. I knew Ron would love it. Gary, who had made the top, said, "I learned a lot today that I will never forget."

Ron came and played the bass. He smiled. I knew we had succeeded. He then spent about an hour and a half testing different wooden endpins until he found the one he liked the best. He had brought a friend, Saadi Zain, to play the bass for him so he could hear it at a distance (not realizing that Robert Kopec would be there).

When he was satisfied with the endpin, we all went into my living room, where all three musicians played a short piece. I listened. The bass had great punch and volume and an amazing clarity and focus. I decided it would take quite a bit of money to duplicate this amount and quality of sound, so I wrote an appraisal for $75,000. Even then it might not be possible to replace the instrument.

Ron Carter and his bass with its Gary Rickman top. (Photo by Fortuna Sung.)

Four separate and distinct external setup adjustments, all of which will be thoroughly examined in later chapters in this book, had brought out the glory of the luthier's work and turned a poor-sounding bass into a thing of beauty of which we could all be proud.

And that is the story of how the bass came into my shop and how it left. The best part of the story may be yet to come, because Ron tells me that the more he plays the bass, the better the sound becomes. He is now playing a one-of-a-kind instrument, one with a new top and a Chuck Traeger setup.

(A year later we did the Krazy Glue Effect treatment; see chapter 4. This setup improved the bass even further.)

And I have learned a lesson. Proper setup is more important to the bass (and string instruments in general) than anything else—and I do mean anything else—in the world, because it gives the most improvement for least cost! And that is what this book is all about.

PART 1

Traeger's Principle and 10 Setup Adjustments

1 Resonance Response Comparisons

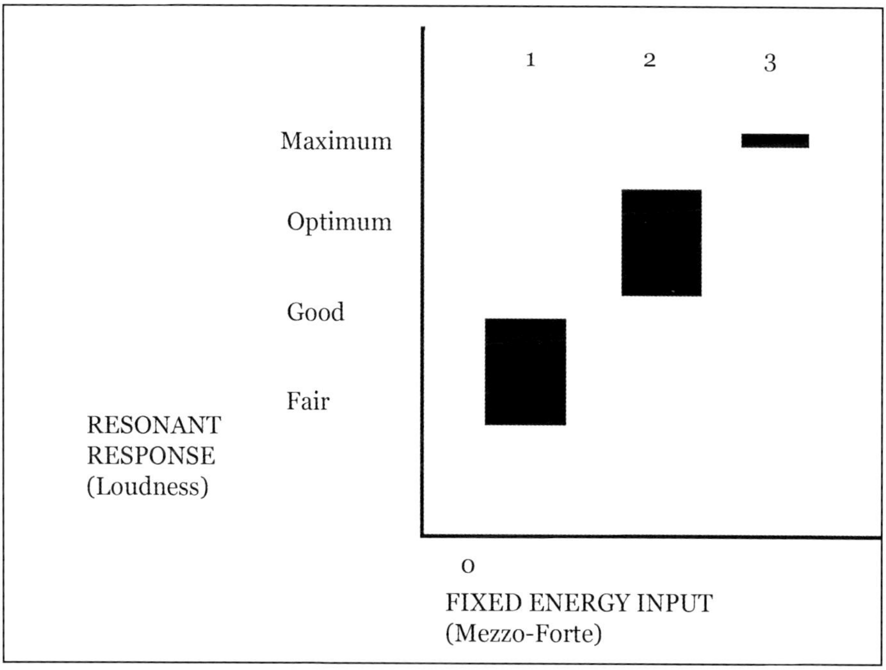

(Illustration by Bill Merchant.)

Column 1 shows how most string instruments respond without optimizing setups.

Column 2 shows the increase in the volume of sound with optimizing setups. You will notice there is a gap in between the top of the "Good" black rectangle and the bottom of the "Optimum" black rectangle. This is because of the immediate and noticeable improvement in volume of sound.

Column 3 shows those rare instruments, which are vibrating too much at a maximum degree, with a resultant "halo" of sound surrounding the basic note. When I wrote *Coda*, I mentioned a bell curve as a visualization tool to see the difference in response between most instruments and those that have had an optimizing setup. I have come to realize that the graph on this page is a better and more accurate way to do this. This graph is an idealized picture of what actually happens to an instrument when a fixed energy input is applied, because every one will have a different amount of response.

I am presenting this graph as chapter 1, because in chapter 2 I will be discussing Traeger's Principle. While reading it, you can refer back to this graph to help you understand what I am saying.

2 Traeger's Principle

A sound is heard when something starts to vibrate. In our case, this is a string. However, if the string was strung between two concrete blocks instead of on a musical instrument, you would hardly hear any tone at all. It is the job of the instrument to resonate this tone. (The dictionary definition of *resonate* is: "the intensification and enriching of a musical tone.") The better it does this job, the louder and better that tone will be. Before you can improve something, you have to know how it works in the first place.

Before I state my principle, I would like to give you a brief history of how it came into being. I had just discovered that the Teflon pads placed under the bridge feet were not helping a bass to sound better because they were helping the bridge; in fact, it was because they were actually helping the top to vibrate more freely, giving the bass a better sound. I was thrilled. Over the next several days, I began to think of other discoveries I have made that had improved the sound of the bass: That a wooden endpin could improve things. How spacing the strings closer together at the nut could help; this was at one end of the bass and then the other. Next, how rounding the edges of the sound post could help more. But it wasn't until the Teflon discovery that things began to come together for me.

Slowly I began to realize that all these were merely parts of a larger whole. What had formerly been a mosaic of separate, apparently disparate discoveries began to turn into pieces of a jigsaw puzzle that, when properly assembled, formed one large and total picture of what was going on with a bass when it is being played.

To understand this, we must first divide the bass into its important component parts. These are the neck/fingerboard, the endpin, the back and ribs, and the top. The first two have primary functions that are practical. The neck/fingerboard allows for the playing of notes of different pitch. The endpin adjusts the height of the bass to a comfortable playing position. But both have a secondary function in the production of sound. The back and ribs' primary function is to support the top, but they, too, have a secondary function in the production of sound. The top has only one function, which is to produce the sound.

But when we look at the top, we must not look at it as one large piece of wood that goes through different motions. We must look at it on a molecular level. We must investigate the motions of the molecules under the bridge feet as they move in three planes. Only then can we really understand what is happening with a bass when it is being played.

It was then that I began, over many years, to formulate, then hone and polish my principle, until it is as you see it as follows. I am very grateful that I have been allowed the time to do this, because I hope that this will be the guide for the all "modern-school" luthiers of the future.

When John Cerullo asked whether Traeger's Principle could cover other instruments beside the bass, I immediately realized it could. So, I changed and expanded the principle to cover all string instruments with an adjustable bridge and a movable tailpiece, or one that could be made so.

Traeger's Principle

When a string instrument is being played, **everything *(every single part)* is *vibrating*** *from one end to the other.*

FIRST COROLLARY: For Optimum Sound to occur, every part of the instrument must be vibrating at optimum level and in sync (in phase) with its neighbors, so that it reinforces the vibrations of its neighbors rather than conflicting with them. A mode match, if achievable, is the ultimate optimizing adjustment, because it synchronizes the vibrations of two major elements of the instrument, both of which, hopefully, are already vibrating at optimum level.

SECOND COROLLARY: Maximum vibration is *not* necessarily optimum vibration.*

THIRD COROLLARY: Anything done to any part of the instrument that makes it easier for that part to vibrate more freely will have a positive effect on the sound and playability. The converse is true. Anything that mutes or inhibits or absorbs and/or dissipates these vibrations is deleterious to the sound.†

FOURTH COROLLARY: Mass and rigidity are the two main enemies of sound. Decreasing mass and increasing flexibility will defeat these two enemies every time.

This principle is equally applicable to all the members of the string family, and any instrument with a movable bridge and a movable (as opposed to rigid) tailpiece, or one that can be made to be movable.

When I wrote that my principle was equally applicable to all the members of the violin family, I eventually discovered I was unnecessarily restricting the principle's reach. Gary Rickman had read my books and remembered what I had written. A customer of his brought in a state-of-the-art Lloyd Loar mandolin with an ebony bridge. Gary took one look at it and said he could make the instrument sound better. He remembered that I had said that ebony was too stiff a wood to vibrate properly, so he replaced the ebony bridge with a maple one. Immediately the sound opened up.

He then took a look at the fixed metal tailpiece and remembered that I had said tailpieces should be free to vibrate. He replaced the fixed metal

*There is one instance where this corollary does not apply. This is the rare instrument where the instrument is so poorly made that it takes a major amount of vibration to get any sound what so ever out of it. In this case, maximum vibration is also its optimum vibration.

†There are a very few instruments to which this corollary does not apply. These are the instruments which are vibrating in area 3 in the graph. They are already vibrating beyond Optimum level and are vibrating so much that they produce a "halo" of unwanted and annoying overtones that surround the main note. In this case, the only thing that can be done is to somehow mute these vibrations slightly to bring the bass back to area 2, Optimum.

tailpiece with a violin tailpiece and the mandolin roared. The customer remarked that he could now play things on it that he never could before.

The moral to this story is that Traeger's Principle can be applied to any instrument with a movable bridge and a movable tailpiece or one that can be converted to be movable!

What you have just read tells you the "why." The rest of this book is dedicated to telling the "how."

3 Setup No. 1—Endpins

When a string instrument is being played, ***everything*** **(every single part), is vibrating,** from one end to the other.

This is one of the very best things you can do for a bass. It may even work for cellos although the longer length of the cello endpin already makes it easier to bend and vibrate.

I am writing about endpins first, because in the early 1970s I got the first hint that changing something in the setup could affect the sound of the bass positively. I had bought a bass that was in unplayable condition, intending to restore it and sell it for a profit. I put the bass back together and bought an endpin assembly that had a ⅝-inch (16 mm) ebony rod for its pin. At that time I thought, erroneously as it turned out, that the better the endpin contacted the floor, the better the bass would sound. So, I bought a piece of solid aluminum rod, fashioned a point on one end, and substituted it for the ebony rod. I thought my bass was now complete, and so I started to play it. The sound was dry and the bass was hard to play. I was dismayed.

I had recently made the acquaintance of Carleen Hutchins, the famed violin acoustics researcher. I decided to take the bass over to her house in New Jersey to see whether she could figure out what was wrong with it. I took it into her living room, took off the gig bag, and had started to play a few notes when she looked at the sharp point of my metal endpin rod and said, "You're not going to play that thing on my floor, are you?"

Fortunately, I had the original ebony rod with me, so I took out the metal one and replaced it with the ebony one. By this time Carleen had gone into another room. I had only played a few notes when she returned and said, "What did you do to the bass?" We could both hear a distinct improvement in its sound. And I could feel a difference in the playability—it was much easier. I surmised it was the difference in endpin rod materials. I have never used a metal endpin since, and that was the beginning of my long, fascinating, and still ongoing journey of discovery.

At that time I realized that the difference in endpin rod materials had something to do with vibrations. I thought it was easier for the wooden rod to vibrate because it was less stiff than metal. But I didn't realize then how or why this had such a positive effect on the sound of the bass.

Less than two years later the company making those endpins changed from an ebony rod to a hollow steel rod. At the same time I discovered that a #2B drumstick fitted quite well into that particular endpin socket. But I didn't know that drumsticks were made of various different woods—for example, maple, hickory, and oak. So, I used whatever I could buy without realizing that each wood would produce a different type of sound in the bass. I continued this practice for some thirty years.

About ten years ago Bill Merchant brought me a carbon fiber rod that fitted that same endpin socket. It gave the bass a completely different quality of sound than the drumsticks I was using. This made me think that other types of wood might produce different types of sound, and I bought half a dozen ⅝-inch

1854 John Lott cello Montagnana model. (Instrument courtesy of Amy Chang.)

(16 mm) rods of different woods. I had mahogany, cherry, black walnut, and ash. I also had drumsticks of maple, hickory, and oak as well as the carbon fiber rod. It was a pretty good collection to experiment with.

The harder woods produce a brighter sound, while the less dense woods, such as mahogany, produce a warmer sound. There was also a difference in the amount of sound. I found that maple generally produced the least volume. And then one day I discovered one particular bass in which maple produced the most sound. I was amazed.

It was then that I realized that something called impedance matching had a great deal to do with the volume that a certain wooden pin produced. Let me give you an example of impedance matching. In a hand-carved bass, spruce is the best wood for a sound post. But in a plywood bass, maple often produces a better sound. The reason is that plywood is stiffer than spruce, so a sound post of maple, also stiffer than spruce, will produces a better sound in those basses. The two stiffer woods, plywood and maple, get along with each other better. That is what I call impedance matching. It is also true that mass of the different woods changes the mode match.

The maple in the rod mentioned earlier was a much better impedance match than any other wood for that particular bass. That is why it sounded better than the other wooden rods.

When I realized the importance of impedance matching on the sound of the bass, I thought I had learned all there was about wooden endpins. How wrong I was! Just recently I have learned two new things in connection with wooden endpins.

It is very important that the endpin socket fit tightly into the hole in the endpin block. Any looseness there will soak up vibrations rather than pass them along properly. Once the socket is properly fitted, the endpin, the socket, and the endpin block become one solid, complex integral part of the bass. It is at this point that the mass of the endpin becomes important, because the endpin block is vibrating also! This was the first new discovery. The greater mass of the metal endpin, as opposed to the lesser mass of the wooden endpin, impedes the proper vibrations of the endpin block–endpin assembly, preventing it from vibrating as easily, with a consequent loss of sound.

Half-inch (13 mm) endpins are impractical because they are so thin that they can snap easily. So, I advocate ⅝-inch (16 mm)-diameter endpins over ¾-inch (19 mm) ones, because their greater thickness impedes its ability to vibrate properly. This is true, but something else is at work here.

When a string is pulled, either by fingers or bow, the top ends of the neck and endpin blocks are pulled slightly together. Upon release they spring back into place. The top of the endpin block is moving slightly in a back-and-forth direction. If you could lay the bass on its back and play it in that position, the tip of the endpin rod would move up and down. But this rod sticking out of the endpin block is more or less temporarily attached to the floor (so the bass won't slip). That means that the tip of the endpin is more or less immobilized. Thus, the only way the endpin block can vibrate freely is for the rod to bend slightly. A ¾-inch (19 mm) rod is too thick to vibrate properly, too thick to bend even slightly. Metal endpins hardly bend at all. They also add unnecessary mass to the block and endpin assembly, making it harder for them to vibrate properly. The easier it is for this rod to bend slightly when the block is vibrating, the less it impedes the ability of the block to vibrate properly. This was my second discovery—the more the block is allowed to vibrate, the more sound you will have.

That may have be all there is to discover about endpins, but I have changed my approach to installing them. I had advocated an endpin assembly with a hollow metal rod that could be removed and replaced with various wooden ones. This idea has two drawbacks. First, the wooden rods don't hold so well—they have a tendency to slip into the bass at exactly the wrong time, generally during a solo. Second, the wooden rod gets pretty beat up by the set screw/metal wafer (that acts as a clutch), eating into the wood. For fixes, see chapter 3.

Nevertheless, get rid of your metal endpin and install a wooden one. Even your tone-deaf Uncle Harry, who couldn't carry a tune in a wheelbarrow, will hear the difference.

Don't be afraid to try different woods. Just because a certain wood works well in your friend's bass doesn't mean it will work well in yours. Don't forget about impedance matching. I had hoped to be able to try exotic woods, but I was never able to find them in dowel form.

EXOTIC WOOD ENDPINS—THREE NONSLIP METHODS

Gary Rickman had the same problem with slipping wooden endpins that many other luthiers have had, so he decided to do something about it. He resurrected a centuries-old method of making endpins that didn't slip. That is wooden endpins of a fixed length with a tapered end. This tapered end fitted into a tapered hole in the endpin socket. They never slip, but can only be of one length. This didn't seem to bother the players of those bygone days. Unfortunately they were all made for ¾-inch (19 mm)-diameter endpins, which I believe are too thick to vibrate properly.

He started making this type of endpin, but with a ⅝-inch (16 mm)-diameter rod, then he began experimenting with different woods.

One day a customer of his walked into his shop carrying a piece of padauk, an African hardwood. He was already using a wooden endpin that he had installed, and had watched and listened as he tried out various different woods until he had found one that was to the customer's satisfaction. Fortunately, the customer had an inquisitive mind and wanted to see whether a padauk endpin would make a difference. So, Gary made one.

When the bass was played, the sound was noticeably louder and clearer. Both Gary and his customer were amazed and pleasantly surprised.

This piqued Gary's interest, and he found a close source of exotic hardwoods that he could fashion into endpin material. His next choice was cocobolo, from South America. This was even louder than the padauk. Next he tried ipe (pronounced *ee-pay*), another very hard South American wood usually used in decks and boardwalks. It was the loudest so far. Finally, he tried African purpleheart wood.

He sent endpins of the four woods to Ron Carter to try. Ron reported that all four made the bass a bit louder but they all produced a bright sound which Ron didn't like, so he went back to the warm sound of black walnut. However, if you want to try, remember that Teflon pads under the bridge feet will soften a bright sound.

What Gary had done was to carry my wooden endpin research to its ultimate conclusion: he found an exotic wood that produced a louder sound than any North American hardwood.

Shortly before Thanksgiving 2014 an old friend of mine, Tony Dominic, and his lovely wifc, Michele, drove up from Pennsylvania to have dinner with us. He is an excellent amateur bass player (and full-time pharmacist). During the course of the evening the talk turned to endpins and their habit of slipping at just the wrong moment. Right off the top of his head Tony came up with a solution that was so simple and practical that it boggled my mind. Here it is—inside the Klengel model endpin assembly is a small metal disk that sits between the wing bolt and the endpin rod. When the bolt is tightened, the disk presses up against the endpin rod supposedly preventing it from slipping. Unfortunately, this is not always the case. Tony's answer to this problem was to drill a hole through the center of the disk, large enough to allow the bolt to pass through without getting hung up. Then, examine the wood of the endpin carefully. You will see that one side of the rod shows the tree growth layers of summer and winter growth. Turn the rod ninety degrees and you will see smooth wood without these layers. Drill a $\frac{1}{8}$-inch (3 mm)-diameter hole deep into the rod here. Tighten the wing bolt until it enters this hole. The endpin will never slip. Draw a pencil line down the side of the rod from the hole to the bottom end of the rod. This will act as a positioning guide for future use. And that is all you have to do. If the wing bolt is not long enough, buy a longer bolt, but it has to be metric thread—6 mm x 1.00—and needs to be at least $\frac{5}{8}$-inch (16 mm) long (available at www.mcmaster.com). Bye-bye slippage. The $\frac{5}{8}$-inch Klengel model endpin assembly can be ordered from Metropolitan Music Co., PO Box 1415, 4861 Mountain Road, Stowe, Vermont 05672, phone: 802-253-4814, e-mail: sales@metmusic.com. It is model no. 6426.

Third method: Ron Carter recommends a bicycle seat clamp to hold the endpin in place. I am not in favor of adding that extra mass to the endpin assembly because I know it will have a slight negative effect on everything, but if you want to sacrifice a little sound for a lot of convenience, be my guest.

Another way to have a wooden endpin. (Photo by Ron Carter.)

4 Setup No. 2—The Sound Post

Anything done that mutes or inhibits or absorbs and/or dissipates these vibrations is deleterious to the sound.

This setup is equally applicable to all the members of the string family. You can round the ends of the sound post in any of the smaller instruments, just do it a bit less.

My sound post discovery did not come in a lightning-flash epiphany. In fact, it took decades of chance observation and moments of wondering before I understood what was happening and why. **But it was my most important discovery, because it taught me how much science has to offer the modern luthier.**

My first observation happened sometime in the 1970s. Famed bassist George Mraz had brought me his bass for some minor gluing. While examining his bass I noticed that the sound post, which I had originally installed, was not upright, but was leaning such that only a small edge of the post was touching both the top and the back. But the bass sounded wonderful. I dutifully straightened the post and placed it back in what I considered its proper position. The bass's sound declined noticeably. I didn't know why, but my motto is: "Don't mess with success." So, I put the post back in its tilted position, and the sound returned to its former fullness. I wondered why for a moment and then forgot about it, thinking it was just a fluke.

A year later I was examining a bass that had been worked on by a luthier by the name of Varvra. He was an excellent workman who had emigrated from Czechoslovakia. He first worked in the shop of Metropolitan Music before opening his own shop just across the Hudson River in New Jersey. He justifiably had a very good reputation. I looked at his sound post and was appalled to see that the ends of the post appeared to have been carved smaller with a pocket knife. But the bass had a wonderful sound, so I left the post in the bass. Again, there was that fleeting moment of wonder.

We now travel in time to the start of this century. I was doing a minor overhaul to a bass. When I was done, I gave a final examination to the instrument, which had an excellent sound, and found something that didn't look right about the sound post, so I pulled it out. I was shocked to discover that the post had ends completely rounded as in the shape of a bullet and that someone had driven a small carpet tack into both ends of the post! The top had been gouged by the tack, but was still in playable condition. All it needed was a properly fitted post. "If the bass sounds this good with this piece of junk in it, what will it sound like with a properly fitted post?" I thought.

I made the post, fitted the ends very carefully to the top and the back, and installed it in the bass. The sound died! I was so disappointed that I called up Carleen Hutchins to discuss this with her. I told her what I had done (and why), and as soon as I told her that I had installed my post she finished my sentence with the words "and the sound died." I was amazed.

She then went on to explain that she had discovered that when the bass is being played, the top and the back exert a twisting motion to the post. I immediately understood the problem.

The larger the motion of the top and the back, the better is the sound. Less motion means less sound. This is my third corollary. Perhaps this is why sound posts that seem to be "too short" to many luthiers give such a full sound to the instrument. More of this later.

The string pressure jams the bass top down tight onto the post. This produces friction between the post and the top and back. It is this friction, which is an impediment to the natural motion of the top and back, with a consequent loss of sound. I can hear you saying, "That little bit!?" Yes, that little bit. When you consider that less than half of 1 percent of the energy that goes into the bass to produce sound ever comes back out as sound, you can understand that even the smallest thing becomes big, especially if that little thing is a negative thing. That is why I especially round the edges of both ends of my posts to produce a bearing area of only ⅝ inch (16 mm) in diameter on each end instead of the standard ¾ inch (19 mm). The smaller the bearing area, the less friction there is impeding the natural twisting motion of the top and back, with a consequent increase in sound. I do not round the ends of the post into the shape of a bullet because it would put a dent in the wood of the top. (This has the added benefit of making it impossible for a tight post to split when removing it, as well as giving the luthier an elegant way of knowing how much has been taken off when sanding the post.)

The size and the shape of the ends of the post after they have been rounded are very important. The shape must be as nearly round as possible. If it were oval, for example, you might change the sound of the bass by rotating the post several degrees. The size must be as close to ⅝ inch (16 mm) as possible—½ inch (13 mm) would probably put a dent in the wood of the top. The easiest way to do this is with a belt sander, but a piece of sandpaper and a sanding block will do. Do not carve or plane, as this can produce a ragged edge.

For smaller instruments, just round the edges of the ends of the post enough to make a smaller bearing area. If the sound is too bright, you can darken it by placing Teflon pads under the bridge feet or by moving the bridge and sound post a little bit toward the tailpiece. If you are afraid that the post will make a dent in the top, try the Krazy Glue Effect setup on the end of the post instead, for a similar result. (For more on this, see the next chapter.)

The idea that it is very important to fit the ends of the post to the top and the back as precisely as possible is an old-school "good enough for my grandfather" myth! It is my pet peeve with luthiers who don't realize what science has to offer the modern craftsman. Luthiers have been fitting posts as exactly as possible for centuries. It is time to stop!

Gary Rickman likens the top of the bass to a bell, because it is when they are vibrating that they both produce a sound. You strike the bell and it produces a note. If you put the palm of your hand on a bell, depending on the size of the bell, you will stop the note entirely or diminish its volume considerably. Strike the bell again. Do it again, but this time put just your fingertip on the bell and compare the sound. There will be only a slight diminishment in the volume of the note. Why? Because less bearing-area friction is touching the bell. Now suppose you put a cap made out of a substance as hard and as smooth as glass on your fingertip and touched the bell and compared the sound to that made with your naked finger. What do you think will happen and why? (For the answer to these questions, read the next chapter.) Gary took my research on freeing up the top to vibrate as efficiently as possible and pushed it to its ultimate conclusion.

More important information about sound posts, plus a brief history of their development:

Before I do any rounding, I make sure that the post is a little loose. Even without the rounding, the bass will sound a little better with a loose post. This is a Bill Merchant discovery. After further conversations with Bill it became evident that there are at least two instances where a short sound post is mandatory. One is in a newly made bass, and the other is in a bass that has had top-off repairs. The reason for this is that in both cases, the top will sag a bit under string pressure after a short period of time, making a regularly fitted post too tight. This is equally true for all string instruments.

Almost half a century ago experimenters were realizing that something might be done to improve the sound of the bass by doing something to the sound post. But what? They first drilled a small hole all the way through a post. This was no mean feat, as it had to be done very carefully so as not to run through the side of the post. There was no improvement. They then made the post in the shape of a long, slender hourglass. Again, there was no improvement. The next move was to carve sets of large, round notches on both sides of the post. One set was in the north–south direction; down below it, the second set was in the east–west direction. Still there was no improvement, because they didn't understand the nature of the problem. It was only the scientific discovery of the twisting motion imposed on the post that dispelled all guesswork.

The two most common sound post treatments—neither seems to have an effect on the bass's sound. (Photo by Bill Merchant.)

As for the length of the post, too tight a post will produce a loss of volume on the A string compared with the other strings. Too loose a post will make the sound muddy. I try to make my posts so that they will just barely stand up with hardly any string pressure on the top of the bass. I prefer a post that is too loose to one that is too tight.

The next time you come across an old-school post, try doing what I have recommended. You will be pleasantly surprised and your customer will be very happy.

One final note about sound posts: most plywood basses produce a better sound if the post is made out of a hardwood rather than spruce. This is because of something called impedance matching. For a more complete explanation of this phenomenon read page 37 of my first book, *The Setup and Repair of the Double Bass for Optimum Sound*. Even a ⅝- or ¾-inch (16 or 19 mm, respectively) hardware store dowel will do just fine.

For maximum sound improvement, rounding the edges of the ends of the post to reduce the bearing area of the post is an improvement that should be done in combination with the Krazy Glue Effect to the sound post.

THE SOUND POST— THE KRAZY GLUE EFFECT

Anything done that mutes or inhibits or absorbs and/or dissipates these vibrations is deleterious to the sound.

For smaller instruments, this may be an alternative setup adjustment you can use in place of rounding the ends of the post if you so choose.

The adjustment described in this chapter is rewarding, but first a story. This chapter almost did not get included in this book. Yet it is probably one of the most important setup adjustments you can make, because it can transform a throwaway bass into a keeper.

I had written all but half a chapter, and I thought I was nearly finished with this book. The unfinished chapter had to do with the saddle. I had a friend in Zurich, Switzerland, called Herbert Kramis. He is a world-class bass player, and he had traveled from Switzerland to study mode matching with me. During his stay he mentioned an adjustable saddle made by a man in Austria by the name of Franz Moser. When Herbert got back home, he sent me one of these saddles.

I was very interested because in a bass that needs a high saddle, there was always the question "How high?" Making such a saddle had always been a matter of trial and error, because there was no way to tell before you started exactly how high to make it. An adjustable saddle was the answer, but no one had made one yet.

The saddle Herbert sent me was made of two pieces. One was a base with a small stairway into which fitted a small piece of wood that could be moved from the lowest step in the stairway to the highest. It was an idea of pure genius. Unfortunately, it had some technical flaws that had to be corrected before I could endorse here. The most significant of these flaws was that the base was unstable, tilting toward the tailpiece when the bass was in full tension.

I corresponded indirectly with Mr. Moser over a period of quite a few months, trying to get the problem resolved. He sent me three different models, each of which got a little closer to the ideal but none of which was perfect. However, during this period a luthier made an important discovery. It is this discovery that is the subject of this chapter. Without Mr. Moser and his adjustable saddle (see chapter 10), this chapter might not have been included in this book.

Gary Rickman was rounding the ends of a violin sound post one day, as described in the previous chapter, when he accidentally spilled some Krazy Glue on one end of it. When it was dry, he put the post back in the violin and forgot about it. The next day, the customer began to play the instrument and was amazed at the increase in power. So, he took out the sound post and put some Krazy Glue on the other end. The result was even more power. He did this to several other instruments, and every time, the result was the same. His next move was to call Ron Carter and tell him about it. They made an appointment to do this to Ron's bass in my shop.

Here is how Gary performs his Krazy Glue treatment. Two essential products are a bottle of thick-viscosity Krazy Glue and a buffer file (available from Metropolitan Music Company, Mountain Road, PO Box 1415, Stowe, Vermont; phone: 866-846-5461; fax: 802-253-9834.) A buffer file is roughly the shape of a doctor's tongue depressor. It contains four small pads of material in which are embedded very fine abrasives, ranging from fine to finer to very fine to extremely fine grit.

Gary first makes the surface of the sound post smooth with a pass or two of the coarsest grit of the buffer file. Next, he puts a couple of drops of Krazy Glue on the sound post. He brushes the surface of the glue with his finger to smooth it out and then immediately wipes the glue off his finger before it has a chance to set. (If it does set, it can be removed with nail polish remover or acetone.) Then, he gives the glued end of the post a small spray of Extreme Power Accelerator, which dries the glue almost instantaneously (or use a hair dryer). If the glued surface isn't smooth, he takes a small pink rubber eraser and bends a small piece of 220-grit sandpaper over the end of the eraser. He sands off any small bumps and spikes from the surface of the hardened glue, because it is important to have as flat a surface as possible, with no small hills or valleys. If the surface doesn't need sanding, he polishes the surface with all four of the buffer file grits, starting with the coarsest. When he finishes, the surface of the sound post top looks as if it has a very thin coat of shiny glass on it. He does this to both ends of the post.

When the post was returned to Ron's bass and the bass was tuned up, the result was amazing. There was instantly a greater degree of clarity to the sound. Ron Carter said the sound wasn't louder, there was just more.

Gary did the same thing to the bridge feet, with the same result. For more about this, read the next chapter. The reason is that a hard surface that can be polished to a mirror finish on the ends of the sound post and the bridge feet presents an almost frictionless bearing surface to the top of the bass. Less friction between the post, the bridge feet, and the top means that the top is freer to vibrate more easily, producing more sound. What he had done was to apply one of the basic principles of physics to the setup of the sound post and bridge feet: he had decreased what is called the coefficient of friction between the bridge feet/sound post and the top.

This should put an end, once and for all, to the old-school luthier's myth that "The better the fit of the sound post to the top and the back, the better off the bass will be."

The most important thing is to produce a surface that looks like a very thin, shiny piece of glass that is extraordinarily smooth. If it takes a few more layers of Krazy Glue to produce this, then do it.

If you do nothing else to your bass, do this setup adjustment. It will more than pay for the cost of the book. One caveat: This does not work on those rare basses that are so well designed and so well built that they are already operating at Optimum level. Instead, it pushes them beyond optimum vibration into maximum vibration, with the consequent addition of a whole host of unwanted sounds. (See the graph in chapter 1.) Remove the Krazy Glue and all will be well again.

One final note: You can substitute any cyanoacrylate glue for Krazy Glue, but do not use Gorilla Glue. It has a different surface finish and does not work. If you go to a hobby shop, you will find cyanoacrylate glue in thin, medium, and thick grades of viscosity. Experiment to find out which works best for you.

All of the violin family instruments, such as this viola, can benefit from the Krazy Glue treatment. (Photo by Ed McCoppin.)

5 Setup No. 3—The Bridge

Anything done that mutes or inhibits or and/or dissipates these vibrations is deleterious to the sound.

This adjustment applies equally to all string instruments with a movable bridge. If you find a round-top guitar or mandolin with an ebony bridge, replace it with one made of maple.

As I reported in the previous chapter, Gary applied the Krazy Glue treatment to both feet of the bridge. When he was done, the bottom of the foot looked as if it had a thin layer of glass on it. The result added even more power and clarity to the sound. He reports that this final adjustment works equally well on any instrument with a free bridge—especially round-top guitars. However, doing the Krazy Glue treatment to both the sound post and the bridge may leave the bass sounding a bit too bright. Place Teflon pads under each bridge foot and this will cure the problem. (See the next chapter.) One note of caution: You will probably have to refit the feet of the bridge to the top because, as careful as you are, the Krazy Glue leaves a slightly uneven surface.

Gary applies the Krazy Glue to the bridge feet in the same way that he does the sound post, with one important addition—it is necessary that the layer of Krazy Glue duplicate the contour of the bridge foot as exactly as possible. If not, the foot will not fit the top as well as it should and some notes on the instrument will suffer.

However, I do not recommend this treatment for bright-sounding basses. It will only make them even brighter with, perhaps, a loss of musicality. But I do recommend this for dark-sounding basses. It will give them more clarity.

There is more to the bridge than this adjustment. Because the bridge has to be handmade by a luthier, it has not fallen into the category of bass furniture. In fact, some thought has been given into improving the bass bridge function. The three-heart model has been more or less discarded in favor of the one-heart model, because this model produces a better sound. The quality of the wood for the bridge blanks has improved. You will rarely see crooked-grain wood in a top-quality bridge blank nowadays. But there are still things that haven't been done.

The first of these concerns the length of the bass bridge feet as compared with the length of the top of the bridge. I have seen infra-red hologram photos of a bridge in motion, and most of the vibrational bending is in the legs. (Refer to my first book *The Setup and Repair of the Double Bass for Optimum Sound*). Therefore, to aid this bending, it is important to make the legs as long as possible in relation to the top. Some luthiers actually carve out some wood from between the legs, just under the heart, to make the legs just a little bit longer. This is a very good idea that I endorse.

As for the thickness of the bridge for bass, I start out with the feet 1 inch (25.5 mm) thick in the north–south direction. This can always be reduced to about ¾ inch (19 mm) thick at a later time, if necessary. I make my tops ¼ inch (6 mm) thick, so as to be thick enough to resist warping but thin enough to allow the string to vibrate optimally. I then adjust the sound post, and if the sound of the bass is too dark, I make the bridge thinner by sanding wood from the front face of the bridge until I am satisfied with the sound. The thicker the bridge, the darker the sound, and vice versa. Sometimes it is necessary only to make the bridge feet thinner to get away from too dark a sound. (For measurements of smaller instrument bridges, see Henry Strobel's *Useful Measurements for Violin Makers.*)

I round off the very top edge of my bass bridges so that the strings sit in notches, which are only about ⅛ inch (3 mm) long in the north–south direction. Were the notches ¼ inch (6 mm) thick, the wood under the strings would act like a mute. I make the notches only deep enough to ensure that the strings do not roll out of the notches. Any extra wood alongside the strings would again act like a mute and dampen the sound.

If a certain bass string sounds too dark in relation to the sound of the other strings, I carve out wood from the underside of the front face of the notch facing the bridge. This reduces the thickness of the wood bearing directly under the string to about 1⁄16 inch (2 mm). This will produce a brighter sound in that string.

Finally, it is very important for the luthier to determine exactly where the bass bar is in each bass. I don't know how many times I have seen a bridge in which the feet were too close together to efficiently pump the bass bar up and down. I have seen some where the center of the E string foot of the bridge is as much as ⅜ inch (9.5 mm) inside and away from the center of the bass bar. The luthier who made that bridge saw a three-quarter-size bass, picked up a three-quarter-size bridge blank, and set to work. The center of the E-string bridge foot must rest directly over the center of the bass bar to function efficiently as a piston driving the bass bar up and down.

There is what I call the heart of the sound area of the top, where you can install a bass bridge without losing volume. This area is no more than ½ inch (13 mm) wide in the north–south direction. This area is centered on an imaginary line drawn between the two inside notches in the F holes. At the north end you will get a brighter sound, but the bass will be slightly stiffer to play; at the south, a darker sound. Talk to the owner of the bass to ascertain what kind of sound he or she desires. Between moving the bridge and moving the sound post, you will probably get it exactly right.

6 Setup No. 4—Teflon

When a string instrument is being played, *everything* **(every single part) is vibrating,** from one end to the other.

This adjustment applies to all string instruments with a movable bridge. For smaller bridges, cut the Teflon pieces to size.

I wrote rather extensively about Teflon pads under the bridge feet and how and why they improved the sound of the bass in my second book, *Coda*. So, I am not going to burden you here with a reprise of all that material. Instead, in case you haven't read that book (or even if you have), I am going to share with you just some highlights about the discovery and what it did for my thinking about bass sound.

In the late 1980s or early 1990s Ron Carter showed up, bringing with him a man from Detroit. This man brought with him several pieces of Teflon material of different thickness and different degrees of flexibility. He claimed that the Teflon helped the feet of the bridge to configure to the shape of the top better and that was why the bass sounded better. The soft Teflon of 0.008-inch thickness proved to be the best. As soon as we put it on Ron's bass, the improvement in sound was so remarkable that Ron and I immediately looked at each other in amazement because we

Teflon can be put under the bridge feet for a warmer sound. (Photo by Bill Merchant.)

weren't expecting anything. Not only was the sound louder, but it had added the warm quality of a much more expensive instrument.

Since then Ron has been using the Teflon pads on all his basses with excellent results. The man from Detroit went back home to get a patent for his invention and to try out his Teflon pads on the basses of the Detroit Symphony. Unfortunately for him, he was unable to get a patent, and he was trying out his pads on exactly the wrong type of instrument. These were basses of such quality that the pads showed only a modest, if any, improvement in sound quality.

The reason behind this minimal showing was that the basses were near or in the top of area 1 in the resonant response comparisons shown in chapter 1. They were already vibrating close to Optimum level. That is why there was only a small improvement in sound quality.

At the time of this discovery Carleen Hutchins and I both thought the improvement was because the Teflon was doing something positive to the bridge. In fact, Carleen had already improved the sound of the bass by slightly rounding the feet of the bridge in the north–south direction, thus accidentally reducing the bearing area of the bridge feet.

It was only many years later that I discovered this was not the real cause for improvement. I had given up dealing with the Teflon because the results were so uneven, depending on the quality of the bass, and because then I did not understand what was really going on.

As I wrote in chapter 3 of *Coda*, one day I had an epiphany while thinking about the improvement in sound that inserting Teflon pads under the bridge feet makes. It was then that I realized that it was not the bridge that was being helped, but the top! The top was now able to vibrate more freely, with a consequent improvement in sound.

A further benefit is that they will cure an instrument that has developed a bright sound as a result of the Krazy Glue treatment. They are also the answer to an instrument that is too bright no matter where you put the bridge and/or the sound post.

I began to think about all the other discoveries I had made that improved the sound of the bass. That a wooden endpin could improve things. How spacing the strings closer together at the nut could help; there was one end of the bass and then the other. Also, how rounding the edges of the sound post could help. This was in the middle of the bass. But it wasn't until I discovered how Teflon could help the top vibrate more easily that things began to come together for me. I began to realize that all these separate, apparently disparate discoveries were related to one another. What had formerly been a mosaic of separate discoveries solutions began to turn into different pieces of a large jigsaw puzzle that, when properly assembled, formed one large and complete total picture of what was actually going on with a bass when it was being played.

It was then that I began to formulate my principle that when a bass is being played, *everything* is vibrating . . . and for Optimum Sound to occur, everything must be vibrating at Optimum level and in sync with its neighbors.

Over the last few years I have honed, polished, and expanded my principle until it is as you now see it in chapter 2. I am very grateful that I have been allowed the time to do this because I hope that this will be the guide for all modern-school luthiers of the future.

7 Setup No. 5—Mode Matching

For Optimum Sound to occur, every part of the instrument must be vibrating at optimum level and in sync (in phase) with its neighbors so that it reinforces the vibrations of its neighbors rather than conflicting with them. A mode match, if achievable, is the ultimate optimizing adjustment, because it synchronizes the vibrations of two major elements of the instrument, both of which, hopefully, are already vibrating at optimum level.

This adjustment applies to all the members of the string family. Treat the smaller instruments exactly the same way as described for the bass.

I have been giving considerable thought to mode matching since I wrote about it in *Coda*. I won't go into those details here; instead, I will give you a short lesson. A mode of vibration produces an audible note in something. If it is a solid, such as a xylophone block, you will hear that note. If it is enclosed air, as in a bottle, you will hear that note when you blow across the bottle mouth. If you can match any two such notes (wood or air) in the instrument, you will hear a definite increase in volume when played. For a complete discussion of this adjustment, read about it in *Coda*.

One of the biggest improvements in volume comes from matching the note of the body of the instrument, B0 (which is changeable), to the enclosed air in the instrument, A0 (which is unchangeable except by reducing the height of the ribs and or cutting the body down). However, to determine the pitch of A0 in a bass, you need to buy three separate pieces of electronic equipment. To make such a match, you may have to do considerable work to the neck/fingerboard. This work is irreversible. So, I have decided not to use this match here.

What I recommend for string instruments is to match the tap tone of B0 to the tap tone of the tailpiece. It does not require a lot of electronic equipment, is not an irreversible repair, and requires only a little time and effort. You can do this by raising or lowering the pitch of the tailpiece until there is a match. There are other matches you can make, but this is the simplest and most rewarding.

To determine the pitch of B0, first thread a dry, heavy cloth between the strings, above the bridge but before the fingerboard, such that they cannot vibrate. Then, tie a heavy cord around the neck of the bass at the nut. Suspend the bass completely in air. Now, tap the end of the fingerboard, or the ears of the scroll, to produce a note. See the photo. You can lower the pitch of B0 by dressing the fingerboard or thinning the neck. You can also lower it by adding a weight to the end of the fingerboard. You can raise the pitch of B0 by shortening the fingerboard or carving out some wood from the underside of the board near the end of the board. However, in that case, you will have done something irreversible and which I do not recommend.

To hear the note of the tailpiece, just tap it about its center. You can raise the note of the tailpiece several ways: You can shift to a lighter tailpiece. You can shorten the hanger cable, but do not do so to the point where the distance between the point where the cable emerges from the tailpiece and where it crosses the saddle is less than 1 inch (25.5 mm), as this will prevent the tailpiece from vibrating properly. You can also put the hanger cable pieces farther apart over the saddle. For smaller instruments use the Sacconi adjustable nylon tailpiece cable to change the length of the cable.

You can lower the note of the tailpiece by going to a larger, heavier model, or by extending the length of the hanger cable, or by placing the hanger cable pieces closer together over the saddle. Do not try a match

A bass hung so you can tap it to determine B0. (Photo by Bill Merchant.)

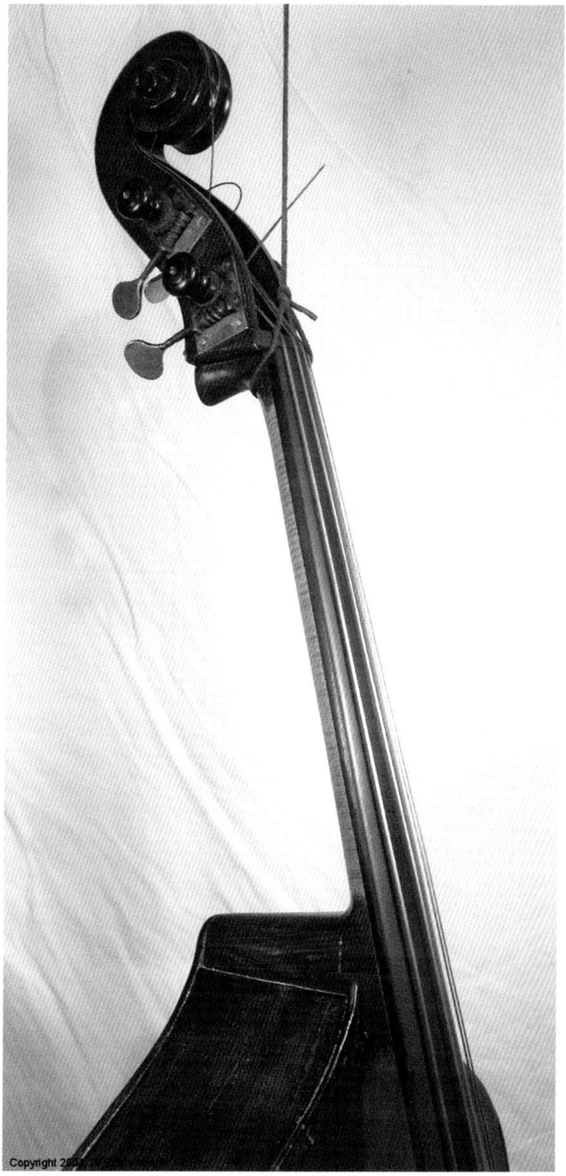

where the interval between the two notes is more than three semitones apart. This distance between tones is too great to achieve a match.

Any time you add weight, either to the tailpiece or the neck/fingerboard, you will shift the tone in a darker direction. You will also decrease the volume slightly.

With Ron Carter's bass, the difference was three semitones. I wanted to achieve a bright sound that was as loud as possible, so I chose a quarter-size tailpiece with a very long cable hanger wire. I achieved the match, and the result was a loud, clear, well-defined sound—exactly what Ron wanted.

I have come to the conclusion that the best, safest, and easiest way to make a match is between B0 and the tailpiece tap tone. When Herbert Kramis came from Zurich to study mode matching with me, he brought with him an excellent bass. After tailpiece mode matching, he left with a superb instrument. This was one of the matches I did to Ron Carter's new bass. He loved it.

At first you will find that it is hard to distinguish the tap-tone note at the end of the fingerboard (or at the ear of the scroll) for B0 and the tap-tone note of the tailpiece at its center from a dull thud. Sometimes a tuner will help. But don't be discouraged and don't give up. Keep on tapping and eventually you will begin to hear the note. I have seen this happen time and again in my shop. If you can achieve a match you will be thrilled with the results.

Good luck.

8 Setup No. 6—The Tailpiece

When a string instrument is being played, *everything* (every single part) is vibrating, from one end to the other.

This adjustment applies to any string instrument with a movable (as opposed to rigid) tailpiece, or one than can be made movable (round-top guitars and mandolins). Remove the fixed, rigid tailpiece and replace it with a movable one.

Ibanez guitar modified with flexible ebony tailpiece. (Photo by Robert Kopec.)

I am starting this chapter with a photo of an Ibanez electric guitar. As you can see, thc fixed, rigid, metal tailpiece has been replaced by a movable ebony one. The owner hadn't played it because the sound was dead.

I took one look at the guitar and told him, without making any promises, that I thought I could fix the sound, because I had noticed the tailpiece. The third corollary to Traeger's Principle states that if you can make any single part of a string instrument vibrate more freely, that will have a positive impact on the whole instrument. At this point the third corollary was just a prediction. Its veracity had never been proven. Replacing the fixed, rigid, metal tailpiece with a movable ebony one would be the acid test.

The test turned out to be a complete success. The sound was immediately and noticeably louder, and the dead-sounding fundamental had been replaced with a series of lively overtones. The musician playing the guitar also reported it was easier to play.

This is proof positive of the validity and strength of Traeger's Principle. That is why it is here.

Round-top guitar makers, acoustic and electric: You will make a better-sounding instrument if you discard the fixed, rigid, metal tailpiece and replace it with a light, mobile one.

The tailpiece is not a part of "instrument furniture"! It has a very important role to play in the amount of sound and the type of sound that the instrument produces.

While it is a very important part of mode matching, it is also capable of doing other things. If you cannot do a tailpiece mode match because the modal tones are too far apart, you can still influence the bass in a positive way with the tailpiece.

The tailpiece actually acts like a sound filter. A large, heavy tailpiece will give the instrument a darker sound, but one that is a little less loud than that produced by a light tailpiece. Conversely, a small, light tailpiece will help the instrument produce more sound with a brighter edge. In other words, it all depends on mass. The more mass, the darker and less sound there will be, and vice versa.

David Brownell, my luthier friend and one of the coauthors of my first book, reminds me that there can also sometimes be a sound energy reflection when there is an acoustic impedance mismatch between the bridge and the tailpiece, with an observable loss of sound. This may be corrected with another tailpiece of different mass.

The question of mass was very forcibly brought to my attention when Ron Carter sent me a very light tailpiece made completely of various wires. I removed a standard three-quarter-size ebony tailpiece from a bass and replaced it with the one made of wires. The maker said it would make the bass sound louder. He was correct, but the resulting sound was piercingly shrill and bright. We discarded the wire tailpiece and the idea behind it.

There is a definite need for the so-called compensated tailpiece in which the end of the tailpiece facing the bridge is angled in such a way as to make the string length between the tailpiece and the bridge longer for the strings as you go from the G string to the E string on the bass.

The need for this is simple: The E and A strings have a larger mass per unit length than the G and D strings. If these lower strings are positioned too close to the bridge, the greater mass of the part of the string between the tailpiece and the bridge will prevent this part from vibrating properly, with a consequent loss of sound to the rest of the string. One example—you have reached a mode match with the tailpiece but the distance between the tailpiece and the bridge is less than 7 inches. This is the exact situation that calls for a compensated tailpiece. It will probably sustain the mode match while allowing the lower strings to vibrate properly. However, as with all tailpieces, you must have the correct length tailpiece for your bass to get the advantages of these compensated tailpieces. In other words, you do not want a tailpiece that is too long or too short to produce the proper length of hanger cable between the tailpiece and the saddle. In basses that have an E string with a weaker sound, the compensated tailpiece may help.

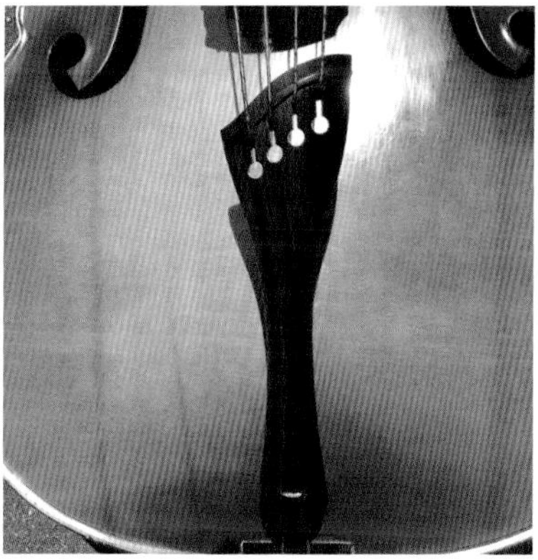

A compensated tailpiece. (Photo by Robert Kopec.)

For sources, go to your computer's search engine and type in "compensated tailpiece" and "double bass," placing each term in double quotes as written here. Do not use the term *bass violin* because the computer will pick out the word *violin* and that will be the end of any bass-specific information. There are two options for holes in the tailpiece for the hanger cable, so be careful when you order. In one, the holes are drilled parallel to the length of the tailpiece and exit out the end of the tailpiece. In the other, they are drilled perpendicular to the length of the tailpiece and exit from the underside of the tailpiece. This means there is a different length of cable between the tailpiece and the saddle. You make your selection based on which wire length you feel you need. Threading the length through the lower end yields a shorter wire than threading it through the holes on the top of the tailpiece would.

There is also another advantage to these tailpieces. Because the string holes in the tailpiece are not side by side as in a regular tailpiece, they can be made closer together without interfering with the structural integrity of the tailpiece. This enables the tailpiece to vibrate more easily because the outside strings do not exert as much lateral force on the tailpiece, impeding somewhat its ability to vibrate. This is the same principle as string spacing at the nut and bridge.

So, don't give up if you cannot achieve a tailpiece mode match. There are these other things you can do to help your instrument. If you want to make your bass a bit louder, switch to a lighter tailpiece. If your instrument is too bright or too dark, you can alter this somewhat by using a heavier or lighter tailpiece, as the case may be.

Finally, here are some tailpiece tips: Never use a solid wire for your hanger cable. It will be too stiff to allow the tailpiece to vibrate properly, and it will eventually break. Never position your tailpiece for bass so that the E-string length between the tailpiece and the bridge is less than 7 inches. That part of the E string will not vibrate and this loss in vibration will cause a loss in sound in the E string. Never position your tailpiece so that part of the hanger cable between the tailpiece and the saddle is less than 1 inch (25.5 mm). You can extend this length to at least 2 inches or more, if desired. Try positioning the cable parts over the saddle as close together as possible. It will enable the tailpiece to vibrate more easily. It may also darken the sound. If you want a brighter sound, spread the cable farther apart. Everything I have written here will help you get closer to the sound you desire. Try them, and good luck.

While proofreading this chapter, I came to realize that I had given you an awful lot of material to think about in a short space.

This material is important to you and your instrument. So, I suggest you take the time and make the effort to reread this chapter several times until you really understand it. When you apply it to your instrument, you will see that it was time and effort well spent.

P.S. I have just read some posts on the Internet that say people have found that a compensated tailpiece seems to help diminish or eliminate wolf notes and gives the instrument a better sound and easier playability.

I know that wolf notes on the bass are almost always between G-flat and A-natural. I also know that the part of the E string between the bridge and the tailpiece can be tuned in that range by shortening or lengthening it. If it can be tuned to exactly the same pitch as the wolf note, it will absorb a lot, if not all, of the wolf note's energy and eliminate it, or at least reduce it.

As noted earlier, it is possible with compensated tailpieces to set the holes for the string closer together. This reduces the lateral force of the outside strings, which force reduces the ability of the tailpiece to vibrate as easily as possible. The easier it is for the tailpiece to vibrate, the easier it will be to play the bass.

These are my opinions. However, if the compensated tailpiece has a positive effect on the sound and playability of the instrument, leave it alone. My motto is: "Don't mess with success!"

9 Setup No. 7—String Spacing

Anything done that mutes or inhibits or absorbs and/or dissipates these vibrations is deleterious to the sound.

This adjustment applies to any string instrument with a nut.

After my endpin discovery, my second discovery—that a change in setup could have a positive effect on the sound of the bass—came just as accidentally as the first, and no more than a year later.

I had a customer who had a bass with a very bad wolf note. The instrument was a good average-grade, workman bass that was a bit hard to play. The wolf didn't make the bass unplayable, just a little uncomfortable. I had in mind an experiment that I wanted to try, so I asked him whether he would loan me his bass so that I could try it. I assured him that I wouldn't harm the instrument and that I would return it to him in the same condition as when he loaned it to me. He agreed.

What I wanted to see was whether an overwide versus an underwide bridge with appropriate sound post setting would make a difference in the wolf note.

I set to work and first made a bridge that was at least ¾ inch (19 mm) too wide. I then adjusted the sound post so that it sat in the correct position relative to the foot of the bridge. I played the bass, and there was no difference in the wolf note. It was just as loud and annoying as before. So, I discarded that idea. It didn't work.

I next made a bridge that was so narrow that the outside edge of the E-string foot was just barely over the inside edge of the bass bar. Again I adjusted the sound post to a proper position relative to the bridge foot. When the bass was played, the wolf note still hadn't changed at all.

It was a negative finding, but at least it told future researchers not to go there. I wasn't totally discouraged. Examining the bass, I discovered that the nut was very poorly made. Not only were the strings too high off the fingerboard, but they were very unevenly gapped. So, as a present to my customer for his kindness in loaning me his bass, I decided to make him a nice new nut.

I very carefully spaced the strings at ⅜ inch (9.5 mm) apart, measured string center to string center. I also made sure that the strings were just barely over the fingerboard and that about two-thirds of the string was showing above the groove in the nut rather than in it. Were they any deeper in the nut, the wood alongside the string would act like a mute. It was a nut meant for the best sound and to make it easier for the player's left hand.

I played the instrument and immediately noticed that the bass was noticeably easier to play with the right hand and a bit louder. My first thought was, "Why?" I realized that the strings were much closer together overall at the new nut than at the old. But why should this have made a difference? It took me a while to figure this out, and then one day I passed a cell tower and looked at the stays on the tower. The farther distant from the tower that they were at the base of the tower, the less the top of the tower was able to move. Good for cell towers, bad for bass necks.

When a string is pulled, the neck goes through a combination of four different simultaneous motions. The neck pulls forward as one straight piece without bending, pushing the top of the neck block forward in response to the increased tension of the string. The neck also bows forward in response to the same increase in tension. But these motions do not concern me for the purpose of this chapter, because these two motions are controlled solely by the combined thickness of the neck/fingerboard and there is absolutely nothing you can do to the nut that will make any difference in these motions.

However, the neck also is pulled sideways as a unit without bending, because the string is pulling it in this direction. Again, it also bows sideways in response to this sideways pulling. The farther apart the strings are at the nut, the more they act like the stays on the cell tower, impeding this natural sideways motion of the neck. Third corollary: "Anything done that mutes or inhibits these vibrations (motions) is deleterious to the sound (and playability)." The closer the strings are, the easier it is for the neck/fingerboard to go through its natural bending and bowing motions. This greater, easier mobility means less resistance to the right hand—easier playing.

Much later on I discovered that the closer the strings are spaced at the bridge, the better the bass will sound, for the same reason. I was restoring an old French bass for the Metropolitan Museum of Art. It had been originally built as a three-string bass and later converted to four. The museum wanted it returned to its original configuration. When I was done with that, the museum had found someone who made three gut strings as in the old style. When the bass was set up with these strings, I wasn't expecting much. But when it was played, I was amazed at the sonority of the instrument. I realized immediately that not only were the three strings closer together at the nut, they were also closer together at the bridge This presents less impedance to the natural sideways motion of the bridge. That is one of the reasons the old bass sounded so good!

The moral to this story is to space your strings as close together as possible at the nut and the bridge. Your instrument will benefit by it, and so will you.

As an afterthought, let me describe to you how the aforementioned motions of the neck affect the sound of the instrument. When the string is pulled, the neck goes through those motions. When the string is released, the neck pops back into its original configuration. As the string vibrates, the neck goes through these pull-and-release motions very rapidly. It is vibrating.

A neck that is too thin will bow more than it should, instead of pushing the neck block forward as discussed, decreasing the vibrating motion of the neck block. This decrease in motion transferred to the neck block is subsequently transferred to the top, with a consequent loss of sound.

A neck that is too thick, besides being too thick to bend or bow at all and therefore vibrate properly, will also be too heavy in mass to vibrate at optimum condition. The extra mass of so thick a neck acts like a damper on the vibrations of the neck, with a further loss of sound. I hope this explanation helps in your understanding the importance of an optimum thickness for the neck/fingerboard.

In between having a neck that is too thick and one that is too thin, there is an optimum thickness, which will transmit the vibrations of the strings to the body of the bass at an optimum level. See chapter 18, "Useful Measurements," for a discussion of this thickness.

TUNING IN FIFTHS

Tuning in fifths will also open up the sound of the bass and make it easier to play. The tuning is C–G–D–A from the bottom up—this has been reported to me by two different players. I have no idea why this happens, nor did Carleen Hutchins, but I mention it here for some future acoustic researcher to discover.

10 Setup No. 8—The Saddle

This adjustment probably applies only to basses which are stiff, tight, and hard to play.

There is no doubt about it: Your bass is stiff, tight, and hard to play. You have checked the sound post to make sure it is not too tight. You have checked the string spacing at the nut and the bridge to make sure that neither is too wide. Everything seems to be okay, yet the bass is still stiff. This can result from several causes, a neck set that yields a bridge height of 7 inches or more being the most common.

For any of these causes, there is a remedy: make and install a high saddle. But how high? That is a good question. You can make a really high saddle and gradually cut it down, but how do you know when to stop? Too low and the bass will still be stiff and hard to play. Too high and the sound will be muddy and unfocused.

Well, there is an answer; which was brought to my attention a short while ago by a friend in Germany by the name of Jonas Lohse and by Herbert Kramis, a bass player and band leader in Zurich, Switzerland. They wrote to me about an adjustable saddle invented by an Austrian, Franz Moser.

I am indebted to Herbert Kramis because he not only sent me one of the Moser saddles, but he also acted as interpreter and negotiator with Mr. Moser over a period of several months while we fine-tuned his invention.

For more information on Herbert and his band, go to your web browser and type in "www.herbertkramis.com."

I am also indebted to Robert Kopec, for his help in testing Franz Moser's designs until we found the perfect one.

As you can see from the pictures in this chapter, the Moser Adjustable Saddle consists of two pieces. There is a base that sits where the original saddle did, which contains what looks like a three-step stairway. There is a much smaller piece of wood that can be placed on any of the three steps. These three steps give you three different heights for the movable little saddle, and you can then choose the one most suitable for your bass.

Adjustable height saddle, both off and on a bass. (Photos by Bill Merchant.)

This device is truly a work of genius and I applaud his ingenuity. A note of caution: This device is not for all basses. It is useful only for those basses that are stiff, tight, and hard to play. For basses whose neck set yields a bridge height of 7 inches or more, it is by far the best remedy.

Mr. Moser has made other accessories for the bass. Write or e-mail for a catalog.

For prices and shipping details, contact Franz Moser, Kinostrasse 5, 3680 Persenbeug, Austria; phone +43 676 55 66 714; e-mail: mpm@gmx.at; web: www.moser-mpm.com.

11 Setup No. 9— The Fingerboard

Anything done that mutes or inhibits or absorbs and/or dissipates these vibrations is deleterious to the sound.

This adjustment probably applies only to basses.

Even the fingerboard can have a small but noticeable impact on the sound of the bass.

The curve on a well-dressed fingerboard is very important. I consider it as being two curves. There is the long curve from the nut to the end of the board, the relief; and there is also a short curve under every note on every string, the short or local version of the long curve. The relief should not be too deep or too shallow. If it is too shallow, a great many of the notes will buzz and the bass will lack bottom end, the fundamental and first partial mode of vibration. If it is too deep, by the time you are playing at the octave, you will have to use so much energy to press the string down that you will not be able to play fast, and the bass's sustain will also suffer.

For the long curve, the distance between the string and the fingerboard should be about ⅛ inch (3 mm) at the octave. For classical players, this can be a bit more.

The short curve is the more important of the two. There must be no hills and valleys, which will cause a buzz. If the note is in a valley, the string will buzz against the hill just ahead of the valley. No matter what note is being played, the fingerboard must be curved under that note. I test by holding a 7-inch straight-edge metal ruler against the string, with the straight edge resting perpendicular to the board. On the side away from me, opposite the straight edge, I hold a light. A perfectly dressed board will show a small ribbon of light from one end of the straight edge to the other. If there are any hills or valleys, the light will show them up immediately, as shown in the picture, and these can be corrected.

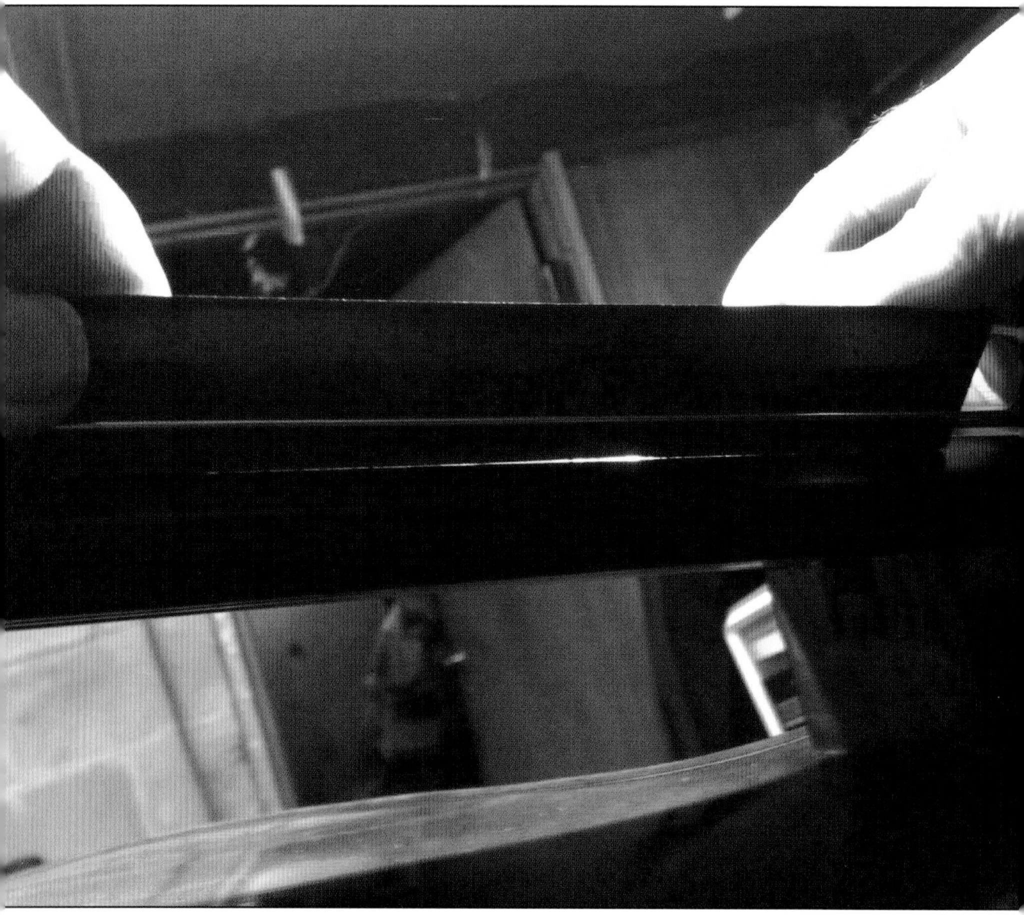

Using a light and a 7-inch straight edge to see fingerboard problems.
(Photo by Robert Kopec.)

Chuck works on the fingerboard. (Photo by Robert Kopec.)

The light will also show flat areas on the board. These are areas in which there are no hills or valleys, but also no curve. If a note is played on the board in a flat area, the note will probably not buzz because it is not behind a hill, but it will lose some of its center and some of its sustain. The reason for this is simple. With a perfectly curved board, the board is curved away from in front of the note. This is not the case with a flat area. The string directly in front of the note will be resting for a short distance directly on the board. This meeting of board and string will produce a slight damping of the string vibrations, causing a slight loss in tonal center and sustain. The flat area must be deepened just enough to introduce a slight curve at this point.

So, for the best sound and the longest sustain, the board must have a slight curve under every note. Don't settle for anything less.

If the board has too deep a curve, it may be fixable. If the board is old and thin from many dressings, the only way to fix a too-deep curve is to replace the old board with a new one and have a proper curve planed in.

However, if the bass has a relatively new board with sufficient wood, the depth of the curve can be adjusted. Plane down both ends of the board for about 8 inches or so of their length and about ⅛ inch (3 mm) or so in depth at the ends of the board, gradually thinning your cut as it gets closer to the middle of the board. (These measurements are approximations based on the depth of the existing curve. You may have to use more or less.) Then, gradually work in the new shallower curve from the newly planed ends to the center of the board. Your customer will be very happy with the final result.

12 Setup No. 10—Tuning Machines and C Extensions

Anything done that mutes or inhibits or absorbs and/or dissipates these vibrations is deleterious to the sound.

This chapter could be Setup No. 11, because it can change the sound of the bass slightly but noticeably. However, it is much more important as an aide in achieving another setup—mode matching. So, that is why I am including it here, after Setup No. 9.

The weight of the tuning machines is very important to the sound of the bass. The heavier the machines, the more they will act like a mute to damp the sound.

Consider the neck and scroll as if they were a baseball bat. When a baseball player is in the batter's circle, he will often put a weight on the end of his bat and then swing the bat. The weight slows down his swing, but when he removes the weight, he feels that he can swing the bat faster. The weight is good for baseball players, not bass players.

The weight of heavy typewriter-type C-extension machines slows down the motion of the neck/fingerboard with a resulting loss of sound. However, it also lowers the note of B0.

That is why I prefer a fingered C extension rather than the old-fashioned typewriter-type machine. The weight of all those metal mechanisms to press the string down to play a note acts like a mute to the bass. The lighter-fingered C extension, without the weight of all that metal, is much better for the sound of the bass.

There are currently on the market so-called fine-tuning machines. These have a large, heavy brass wheel with many cogs. You turn the handle of the tuning machine when tuning up and the large wheel rotates only slightly, giving you much more control of how much you are changing the tension of the string. However, the extra mass reduces volume. Good for tuning, bad for sound. It also lowers the note of B0.

I prefer the individual single tuning machines that have a lightweight plastic spindle for the string. These machines add the least amount of weight to the end of the neck/fingerboard, helping to produce more volume. They also raise the note of B0.

As I mentioned before, you can use these different weight machines to your advantage when you are trying to do a mode match. Experiment until you get the sound you like.

A fingered C extension. (Photo and extension by Bill Merchant.)

PART 2

Repair (Internal) Adjustments

13 Repair Adjustment No. 1—Decreasing the Size of the Neck Block

This adjustment applies to all members of the string family.

While this chapter doesn't have any information about a setup, it does discuss something that will make the instrument better sounding and easier to play. That is why it is here. However, it is aimed directly at instrument makers and repairers rather than players, as you will see shortly.

As a general rule hand-carved musical instruments are made of spruce and maple. Sometimes you will see sycamore or beech wood in necks and pear wood or poplar in backs and ribs, especially in basses. Famed nineteenth-century American bass maker Abraham Prescott and his successors used pine for their tops. I even saw one top made of fir. These basses have plenty of fundamental but not much attack. Although pine and fir are similar in density to spruce, only spruce is flexible enough to bend but stiff enough to snap back into its original configuration rapidly and with little force. This is a high Young's modulus, the measurement of decompression after compression. If it did not have this latter attribute, the bass would sound mushy or "boomy." This is the same reason that classical pianists prefer a stiff action on their pianos. It enables them to play fast and cleanly.

With that thought in mind, let us examine the motions of the top. When the instrument is being played, the top goes through many different motions, in all three planes. I am not concerned here with these motions. Rather, I am interested with what I call the primary or starting motions that the top undergoes when a string is pulled and before it is released, because **the larger these motions can be made, the louder the note will be.**

Pull the E string on a bass as far as you would if you were going to play the loudest E note you could, but don't let it go because we are not interested in sounding a note; you want to see what happens to the top when you do this. If you will look carefully as you pull the string, you will probably see the top of the bass on the E-string side depress slightly. This is a primary motion and the largest and main motion of the top of the bass before it is played. The larger this motion is, the farther the top will have to go before assuming its original position. The farther it has to go, the louder the note will be.

Now, let the string go. You will hear the note, but the top has snapped back into position so rapidly you will probably not see it actually doing this. If it went back into its original position very slowly, you might not hear any note at all.

Gary Rickman suggests that this might not be the only primary motion the top undergoes. He knows that when the string is being played, the vibrations of the string are passed on to the neck. Furthermore, when the neck vibrates, these vibrations are passed on to the top of the instrument.

He began by examining the way the neck is fastened to the body on a violin. The neck butt fits closely into a slot in the neck block and is glued there. The neck block is glued to the ribs and the back of the bass. He realized that the transference of the vibrations of the neck to the top was being impeded by two separate things. The first was the mass of the neck block. The second was the fact that the neck block was rigidly glued to the ribs and the back of the violin.

He reasoned that for the vibrations of the neck to reach the top more efficiently, he would have to reduce the mass of the neck block and reduce the area of the ribs and back to which it was glued. So, he carved wood away from the block, thus reducing its mass. He also carved wood away from the block where it was glued to the ribs and back, reducing this rigid resistance. When he put the violin back together and played it, there was an instantaneous improvement of the sound and playability. His instinct was correct! This will work for all string family instruments.

Carving the neck block smaller had a positive impact on the sound. It has set me to wondering whether those old makers who used what is called a self neck (no neck block) knew something that has been lost. It is something to think about.

String instrument makers, take note. **Perhaps makers should start thinking about string instrument design in a different way.**

14 Repair Adjustment No. 2—Top Plate Regraduation

This adjustment applies to all members of the string family.

A while back I read an article by several luthiers discussing regraduation. They all agreed on two things:

1. *Regraduation* means removing wood from a top where it is too thick and adding wood to the top where the top is too thin.
2. Sometimes it is a good thing to do and sometimes it is a bad thing to do.

Reading between the lines, I deduced that neither these writers nor more than a few of the luthiers attempting this repair really know a foolproof method of doing this where they can guarantee a good outcome. That is because they didn't know the goal of regraduation or how to go about achieving it.

Regraduation is not a matter of guesswork or intuition. It is about having the knowledge that science has brought to lutherie and the technique to implement this knowledge. Science has found that the best sound for an instrument is produced by a top that vibrates at one frequency for as much of the area of the top as possible. This is the goal of regraduation.

Here are two foolproof methods for doing this. One is done by eye, the other by ear. The goal of this repair is to finish with a top in which as much of the area of the top as possible will produce the same note everywhere the top is tapped. The reason behind this is that when the bass is being played, the top needs to vibrate as one integral unit rather than as two or more separate and disparate parts that are vibrating simultaneously but not necessarily in sync with one another. You may not get the entire top to do this. However, if you can get 85 or 90 percent of the top to vibrate at the same frequency (note), you will have improved the sound and response of the instrument noticeably.

Both of these procedures have to be done painstakingly, carefully. This job cannot be rushed. If you want to do this first procedure, read the rest of this chapter very slowly and carefully, because it is a bit complicated to do it right. You will need a sine wave generator, a small amplifier, an 8- to 10-inch speaker, a large ½-inch (13 mm)-thick piece of plywood, some pieces of foam rubber, and some stuff called party sprinkles or glitter. These are very tiny bits of very thin plastic in silver or multicolors. This material is extremely light and will move around easily on the inside of the top when that top is vibrated. Now, measure the thicknesses of the top and draw lines around the areas with about the same thickness. Mark the thickness measurements in pencil. Hook the generator to the amplifier and the amplifier to the speaker. Place the speaker on its back with the speaker, cone face up, on a stable surface, such as a workbench or a table. Take the piece of ½-inch plywood. Cut it about 6 inches wider and longer than the top. Next, cut a round hole in about the center of the plywood, exactly the width of the speaker frame. Center this hole on the speaker frame so that the paper speaker cone does not come in contact with the plywood. Next, cut four pieces of foam rubber, which you will place on top of the plywood in position so that you can rest the upper and lower bouts of the top on these pieces of foam. Cut the foam sufficiently tall so that the top does not touch the plywood. Measure the top thicknesses and mark off the areas with pencil lines and the thickness in millimeters at those areas. Dust the inner surface of the top all over with the sprinkles and place it, this side facing up, on the four pieces of foam.

The goal is to make as much of the top as possible vibrate as one piece. This will produce a noticeable improvement in sound. The sprinkles will tell you where and how much wood to add or subtract. When you are finished and you tap the top anywhere, the entire top will quiver in your hand and produce an audible note.

Now comes the fun part. Turn on the sine wave generator and raise the volume on the amplifier to a moderately loud point. Next, sweep the frequency of the generator note from about 80 Hz to about 140 Hz. The sprinkles will start to move and form various patterns. What you are looking for is what Carleen Hutchins has called the fifth mode of vibration. You will recognize it easily because the sprinkles will form a long, oval pattern on the top, as pictured in the following illustration here. The entire area of the top inside the oval pattern is vibrating as one piece.

At first this pattern will probably be uneven and probably closer to the middle of the top than to the edges. There are two methods of moving the pattern outward toward the edges of the plate as shown in the picture. It all depends on where the problem lies. If the center of the top is more or less the correct thickness (9 to 12 mm), the problem is too much wood outside the oval lines. To make the pattern more even and larger, remove some wood directly from outside that part of the pattern where it curves

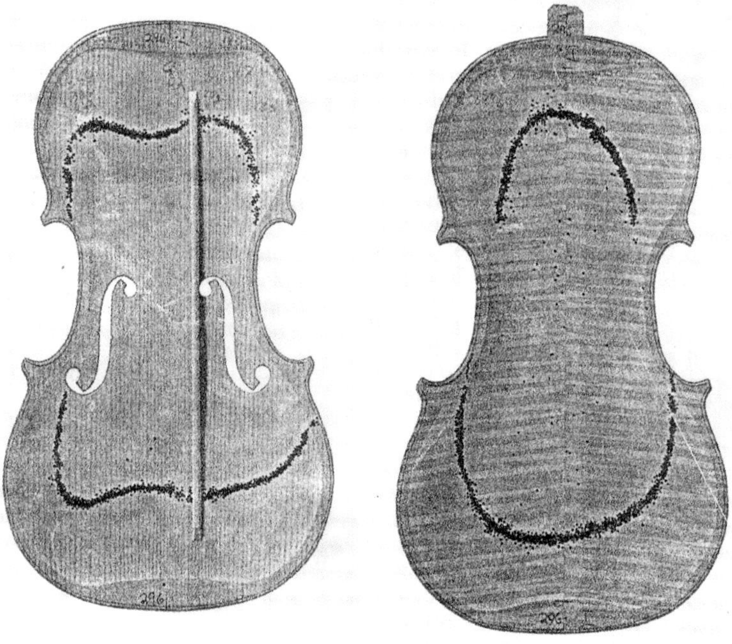

The fifth mode of vibration forms the rings shown with the glitter when excited by the matching frequency sine wave. (Photos by Carleen Hutchins.)

in toward the center of the top. Use a thumb plane or a metal scraper or a piece of glass. (To learn how to make scrapers from glass see page 85 of my first book, *The Setup and Repair of the Double Bass for Optimum Sound*.) To expand the pattern, slowly remove wood from directly outside the edges of the pattern. That is where the top is not vibrating as one piece because the wood there is too thick. If the pattern is very close to the edges of the bass, remove some wood directly inside the pattern where you want to bring the pattern in. If you are careful and patient, you will get a nice oval pattern as pictured. When you tap inside the finished pattern, you will get the same note everywhere you tap. That means that all that area is vibrating at the same frequency, resulting in a better-sounding instrument.

However, if the center of the top is too thin (6 to 7 mm), adding wood there will push the sprinkle lines outward. Now, aren't you glad you measured the top before you started? Tap the top in the center and you will find that the tap-tone note there is lower than the surrounding area when it is too thin. Just as when learning to mode match, you will have to practice your listening until you can distinguish a note from a thud. Tap the area of this lower note gradually outward from the center until you begin to hear a higher note. Now you know the limiting outer edges of the lower note. Mark off this area of the lower tap-tone note with a pencil line. Inside this line is the area where you will have to add wood. Add enough wood to bring that area up to at least 12 mm. This is too thick, but gradually thin out the added wood until the tap tone of the added wood area matches that of the surrounding area. You should make sure that the edges of the added wood are feathered into the original wood. You will find that this has pushed the sprinkle lines farther out from the center. You can now proceed with the rest of the oval lines as described earlier.

This is the scientific method of regraduation and it will tell you exactly how much wood to add or subtract and where. With science there is no guesswork.

You don't have all that electronic equipment? Never mind; there is a second way to do it using only your ears, just as the old masters did. Furthermore, the outlay for materials is limited to two pieces of string and two large rubber bands.

Tie the two rubber bands to the two strings and suspend them from something so that when the rubber bands are placed over the corners of the upper bout, the top will be suspended in midair with the center of the upper bout at about eye level. Now, start tapping and listening. The thicker the wood, the higher the tap-tone note will sound and vice versa. Once again, mark off with a pencil line the areas of the different tap-tone notes, with a penciled notation of the pitch of that note. Assuming that the center is the proper thickness, compare the tone of the center against the other areas. (If the center is too thin, proceed to increase its thickness as described earlier and then continue.) Try to make the tones of the other areas the same as that of the center tone. You will start to remove wood very carefully and slowly, tapping frequently to listen as the tap tone changes, from the areas with a higher tone than the center tone. As you do this you will notice that you are changing not only the tone of the area you are working on but also, somewhat, the tone of the adjacent areas. You may have to go back and forth between areas to get them all to sound the same note before you are done. But if you are patient, you will be rewarded with a top where most of the area will have the same tap-tone note or very close. This method is not quite as accurate as the electronic one, but will still help you produce a top with a very satisfactory result, and it will produce an instrument with a noticeable improvement in sound. It will have been successful, a "good thing" to do.

You will have succeeded because you knew what the end goal was and how to achieve it.

15 Repair Adjustment No. 3—Round Backs

This adjustment applies probably only to basses and cellos.

I know that the following sentence will probably cause some confusion, but here goes anyway. The back, whether round or flat, is the stiffer part of the bass. This *does not mean* that the back is rigid. If it were, it would not vibrate. Stiffer only means less flexible. And it must vibrate for the bass to have any sound at all. The back must be stiffer because it is the foundation upon which the rest of the bass structure is built. Any structure without a good foundation will inevitably fail.

If a round back is too thin, especially down the center seam, the bass will "boom." Booming occurs when a relatively large amount of air is moved around without producing an audible note. This interferes and masks the real note that is being played. In slow passages this does not matter so much, but it makes playing fast passages almost impossible.

Years ago I bought on speculation a bass that had a bad boom. I placed a long-rod joining clamp across the back so that the rod pressed on the center seam. It stopped the boom, but it also diminished the sound of the bass. So, I took the top off. I made 2-inch pieces of ⅛-inch (3 mm)-thick poplar, with the grain running perpendicular to the center seam, enough to run its entire length. I glued all these pieces together along the center seam of the back from one end to the other. This was, in effect, a long strap cleat. When I glued the top back on and played the bass, it no longer boomed. Let us hope you never have to do this.

16 Repair Adjustment No. 4—Flat Backs

This adjustment applies only to basses.

When I wrote my first book, I recommended thinning the crossbars on flat backs from their center to their ends, so that when tapped anywhere along their length they will all produce the same note. I have to admit now that was a mistake. In doing so, two things happened that were not good for the bass. It lowers B0 too much, producing a softer sound in the bass. It also lowers the stiffness of the back, which diminishes the "punch," the initial impact of the notes. Now I only recommend that the centers of all crossbars be tuned to the same note as the note at the center of the central crossbar. If the note of a crossbar is too high, thin the entire bar until you have the correct note. If the note is too low, you will have to add wood to the entire bar to bring it up to pitch. The thickness of each crossbar should be consistent for the entire length of that bar. Live and learn.

On some flat-back basses the crossbars are set into the linings. These bars must be cut short so that there is a gap of at least ⅛ inch (3 mm) between the end of the bar and the lining. This frees the back to vibrate more easily.

The maximum combined thickness of the sound post crossbar and the back must not exceed ¾ inch (19 mm). Any thicker and the back will not vibrate, with a noticeable loss of sound.

For cracks in round or flat backs I recommend poplar strap cleats. The reason for this is that maple expands and contracts with seasonal changes in humidity far more than does the spruce top. I have seen too many back cracks open up again, either popping the small, individual cleats or actually rupturing them. This is also the reason I don't use maple for the cleats—they quickly shrink off the back!

17 Repair Adjustment No. 5—The Kay Plywood Bass

Every serious bass player has a second, backup bass of lesser character and value compared to his or her main instrument. The reason for this is simple: it is a guarantor of the safety and preservation of the player's presumably valuable main bass.

There are more than a few situations to which the player does not want to expose a valuable and fragile instrument. Uncertain travel conditions are certainly among the first. Bad weather is another. A cramped and crowded bandstand can make a player wary. I could go on, but you get the idea.

Quite often the backup bass is plywood, and the most ubiquitous one is the Kay. Like all factory-made instruments, the Kay bass has its ups and downs. Some are surprisingly good, while there are others for which there will never be any hope. But the law of averages is pretty high that you will have a fairly good one.

The Kay bass has some disadvantages and some fortunate advantages, the most important of which is the fact that with only a few changes in setup, the sound of the bass can be improved dramatically. That is why this chapter belongs here.

The disadvantages are that the bass was originally glued together with white glue that over time breaks down to a powder, resulting in a loose neck or an end of the bass bar hanging in the air.

There are two ways to fix a loose neck. One is expensive because it involves removing the neck, shimming up a poorly made tongue-and-groove assembly, and gluing everything back together again. But since the other method works just as well and is considerably less expensive, we will move on to it.

Soak as much hide glue as you can in and around the neck. Make sure the neck is angled down the exact middle of the bass. When the glue has set, drill a guide hole into the center of the outside of the neck butt, close to the bottom of the butt, and insert a deck screw long enough to go into the neck block. Then, cover the screw hole cosmetically.

For the loose end of the bass bar at the bottom of the bass, you do not need to remove the top completely. All you have to do is open up the top on the bass bar side for most of its length and the sound post side to the lower corner block. You can then move the top quite a bit without damaging it, because the plywood will bend. You can now glue and clamp the bass bar in place after you have removed as much of the old glue as possible. Finally, glue a linen patch over the end of the bar as added insurance against its coming loose again. Reglue the top and you are back in business. If the bass bar is loose at the top of the bass, you still may be able to reglue it without taking the top off.

If you have the top off, now is the time to glue on an overlay patch about the size of a human hand and the length of the F holes in the center of the top. Suspend the top by the upper bouts so that it hangs in the air. Tap the top around the center and you will find an area that has a lower note than the surrounding wood. Draw a pencil line around this area because that is where you will glue an overlay patch. Thin this patch so that when finished, the tap tone of the patch matches that of the surrounding top. This will give the bass more punch when played. Bill Merchant suggested this idea to me.

As to advantages to a Kay bass, there are many. After the bass was made, the Kay people did three things that ensured that the bass sounded as poorly as possible. That is why the Kay bass is one of the easiest basses to make sound better: First, remove the solid heavy iron endpin. Then remove the heavy iron endpin socket. You have already removed two sound killers. Install a wooden socket with a wooden endpin and listen to the difference.

At the same time, you should remove the solid metal tailpiece hanger cable and replace it with $\frac{3}{32}$-inch (2.5 mm) flexible metal wire cable or

The stock solid tailpiece hanger and all-metal endpin assembly on Kay and Englehardt basses are bad for the basses' sound. (Photo by Bill Merchant.)

something equally flexible and strong. The bass will heave another sigh of relief. Now, remove the sound post. If you are in luck, the bass will still have its original hardwood post. You can easily spot this because it will have a long, narrow slit in one side of the post. Round both ends of the post to look like the handle end of a drumstick and reinsert the post. Listen again. The bass is getting louder every time you do something. Then do the Krazy Glue treatment to the ends of the post.

If the original post has been replaced with a spruce one, remove it and discard it. Replace it with a hardwood post. Even a wooden dowel from a local hardware store will work. Again, round the ends, drumstick-end style, and insert.

Finally, insert two 0.008-inch Teflon pieces, one under each bridge foot. The sound is now warmer and has some class. You may be playing your Kay more often than you think, thanks to the different setups you just did.

18 Repair Adjustment No. 6—Tuning the Bass Bar

This adjustment applies to all members of the string family.

The top is on your workbench. All the cracks have been cleaned, glued, and cleated. You did some minor edging work. You checked the bass bar to make sure it was glued securely to the top for its entire length, so that there would be no buzzes in the future. You are done. No, not quite. Did you check the bar for proper graduation? I have seen quite a few bass bars in my time, but at least half were not graduated properly. A bass bar is a bar of wood glued to the top on the low string side of the instrument and is generally about three-quarters of the length of the top, measured on a line where the bar is glued. The deepest part of the bar is in the middle, right under the foot of the bridge. From there it tapers slimmer out to the ends of the bar. But how quickly should it taper and how much?

The tap tone of the middle of the bar should be one whole tone higher than the tap tone of the wood of the top right beside the bar at this point. This note should be heard no matter where you tap on the rest of the bar. When a new bar is installed, the middle of the new bar is thinned until a tap-tone note one full tone higher than the tap tone of the top is heard. From there the bar is thinned outward from the middle toward the ends even more, so as to maintain this same note. That is a properly graduated bar. Try tapping the bar you are looking at. Say the note at the center is not quite a full tone higher. Never mind. You will just have to work with what you've got. Tap outward from the center of the bar. If the tap-tone note begins to get higher, thin the depth of the wood at this point until the note is the same. Continue on to both ends of the bar. Then your bar will be properly graduated and will sound the same no matter where you tap it. Bravo!

The inside of a bass top showing a properly shaped bass bar. (Photo by Bill Merchant.)

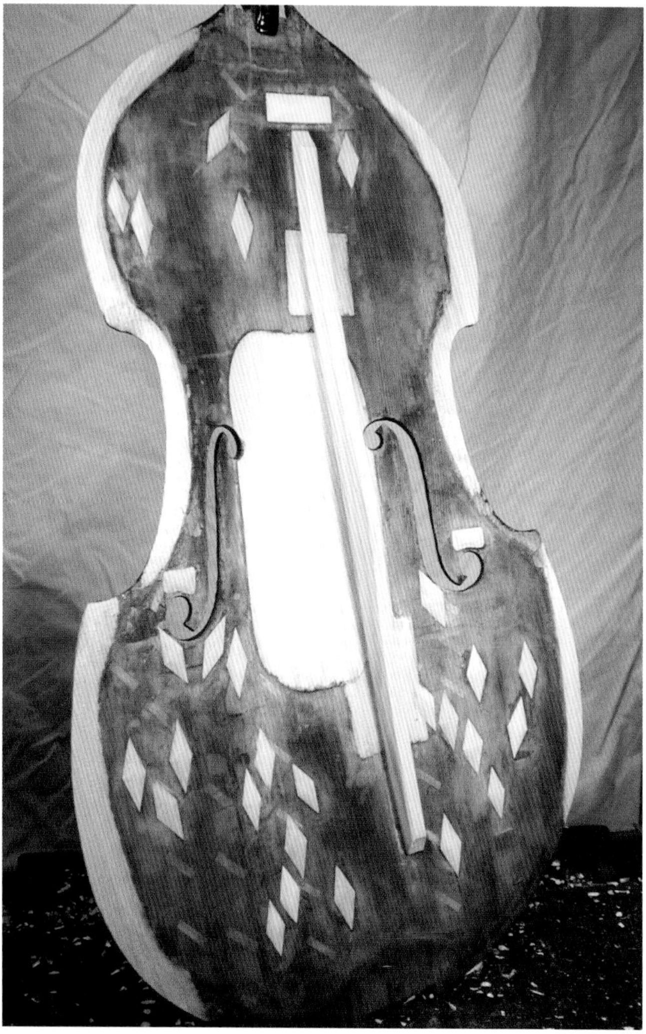

PART 3

Ancilaria

19 The Mystery of Projection

Some instruments are much louder than others. I don't mean under the ear, I mean in the back of the auditorium. This is called projection. As of this writing, June 2014, I am unaware of any research or paper which tells how or why this happens. The reason I am writing this chapter is that I hope sometime, somewhere, someone will read this and try to find the answer. If somebody does, it will be a great help to all the members of the string family.

I have my own theory as to how this happens, but first let me tell you a story. In the early 1960s a bass player friend of mine died suddenly. I took up a collection for his widow, teenage son, and daughter. At Christmastime the union had a package for them, which I delivered. We did what we could to help them through their time of sorrow. While I was there, his widow went to a back closet and pulled out a wreck of a bass. She explained that her husband had hoped one day to have it restored but never did. She gave it to me, telling me that if I ever got it back in playing condition, I was to bring it over and play it for her.

A year or so passed and I had it restored. It was the loudest bass under my ear that I had ever played. I was ecstatic, but as the months went by it gradually lost volume. After a little more than a year, I took it to a different repairman. He took the top off, found some minor problems, and put it back together. No improvement. But I learned that it was made by Tewksbury, a contemporary of Prescott.

I kept playing the bass because it had such a wonderful quality. Finally, I wound up in the show band of the Waldorf-Astoria with it. By now it had lost so much volume that the only way I could play it in tune was to put my ear right up against the neck. Very awkward.

We were playing with Gordon MacRae and his wife, Sheila. One day I found myself standing next to Gordon while we waited for an elevator. He turned to me and said, "That's the loudest bass I've ever heard." I was shocked, but I managed to mumble a thanks. I thought to myself, "Here is a performer who has played in front of hundreds of bands with bass players in them. What was he hearing that I wasn't?" So, I asked the bass player of the intermission band whether he would play my bass on his next set. He agreed.

I went to the front door of the room, about a hundred feet from my bass. I could hear every note loud and clear. I went out into the lobby of the Waldorf through the door where the audience entered. I could hear everything! I walked across the lobby to the door of the sister room to the one in which I was playing. Again, every note! Finally I opened the door of this room and walked all the way to the back wall. I was now almost a full block away from my bass. I could hear every note loud and clear! I was amazed. But I finally had to sell the bass because it was just too hard for me to play in tune.

This all happened before I met Carleen Hutchins. I spoke to her about it, but she didn't become interested until she began to notice that some of her own instruments were projecting more than others. By then she was too advanced in age to do the necessary research on the problem.

Here is what I think happened to my bass over a two-year period. Carleen had written a paper that she called the capstone of her career. I had it reproduced it in my first book, *The Setup and Repair of the Double Bass for Optimum Sound*. I will quote from her article. I have had to change the words slightly because she used the delta symbol for the words "difference of" and I don't have it on my computer. "Violins with a A1–B1 difference of 100 Hz or more are so harsh as to be unplayable . . . Those with a difference in the 60–80 Hz range are liked by soloists for their wide dynamic range and bright projection qualities . . . As the A1–B1 difference decreases below 40 Hz the violins are more and more used by chamber music players and are prized for their smooth tones and easy playing qualities . . . A difference in A1–B1 of less than 20 Hz is found in easy-playing, soft-sounding violins with little power or projection." It is my belief that when Carleen wrote that, she was basing it on her own observations with the instruments right under her ear. Nobody was listening to those instruments at a distance. Little power, yes. Projection?

A1 is unchangeable. The difference occurs as B1 becomes *lower* in frequency and approaches the frequency of A1. The volume gradually decreases. What would happen if B1 became equal to or lower than A1? Would the instrument lose all volume under the ear and start to project more and more? I don't know, but it has me wondering.

20 Don't . . .

This chapter is applicable to the entire string family.

This first *don't* is probably the most important. Don't do your own repair work. The chances of your doing it correctly are probably about 1 in 100. Bill Merchant once quipped, "Some of our best customers do their own work." What he meant was that generally the work was done so badly that for repair work to be done in the future by a knowledgeable luthier, that luthier first had to take the time to undo the customer's bad work before the needed repair work could be started. Time is money, and this means an additional cost to the customer. So, unless you can't get through the gig without doing something, don't do it.

If you have an open seam or a crack somewhere, don't "repair" it with adhesive tape. When the tape is pulled off, it will take some varnish with it leaving an ugly scar on the finish. If you have an open seam that is buzzing, try to put something like a matchbook cover in the opening to push the parts far enough apart so they won't buzz, until you can get it glued.

If you have a tailpiece mode match and you change strings to another brand, test the match to see whether it still is a match. Different strings have different tensions, which can alter a mode match. Don't just keep playing in the belief everything is still okay.

If you have just achieved a tailpiece mode match, don't hang something like a bow quiver on the tailpiece. If you do, good-bye match. Also, don't place a pickup cable holder on the strings between the bridge and the tailpiece. Also, good-bye match.

If you have a mode match involving the neck/fingerboard and the fingerboard needs a dressing, you will have to check the match afterward, because dressing the fingerboard will lower the pitch of B0.

When you install strings on the tuning machines, don't cross the strings in the tuning box. To avoid this, take the loose end of the new string and lead it through the hole in the spindle, aiming the string toward the scroll. Then, take that part of the string and pull it toward the tuning machine you are installing the string on. Next, pull that end of the string under the part of the string that is going to be in tension. Now, start tuning while you hold the loose end of the string in place. You will see that the taut part of the string is jamming the loose end against the spindle. The string will never slip, and you won't have to keep tuning forever just to wind up the last part of the loose string.

Don't forget to check the position of the bridge and sound post occasionally. The chances that they may have slipped out of position during moving are pretty good.

Don't forget to check the bridge for uprightness. After many tunings, the bridge will probably have pulled forward toward the fingerboard. If it is left in this position, it will begin to warp. If you can't get a luthier to pull it back, place the instrument on a table or bed. Stand at the bottom end of the bass. Place your elbows on the top or beside it and grab the top of the bridge with both hands. Now, gradually increase the pulling pressure of your hands while trying to wiggle the bridge a little. Go slowly and gradually because if you don't, the bridge may suddenly fly back toward you and collapse, and the sound post may fall down. Good luck.

Don't leave your instrument in a heated room in winter without a humidifier and a humidistat that tells you the percentage of relative humidity. Try to keep the room humidity at least at 30 percent. Forty percent is better. Twenty percent is dangerous, because the top may crack.

Some things look better on paper than in actual use. Such is the bent metal end pin. Anytime you go from wood to metal end pins you will lose sound, more so if the metal is bent.

Don't take your instrument out of tension unless you are doing it for added safety when traveling. You should tune it down when shipping it in a trunk, to prevent the string tension from causing more damage if something should break. Before I became a show band player, a luthier, and a friend of Carleen Hutchins, I was a jazz player. I knew nothing about the mechanics of the bass, so I thought that I would give the bass and the strings a rest every night by tuning down the strings slightly but not enough to dislodge the sound post. A company decided to record the band I was with, so I got to the recording studio early to tune up again because I knew it would take a bit of time for the strings to stretch out again. I didn't want to be tuning up in the middle of a recording. Three hours later the engineer told me the recording had gone very well but he added that the sound of my bass kept changing during the entire session. After that, I never took my bass out of full tension.

21 Motions of the Top

When the string is pulled, the extra tension exerts a compressive force on the neck block and on the endpin block as well. In response to this force, the top ends of the two blocks are pulled together, producing a compressive force on the top of the instrument. The low-string side has compressed. The only way the top has to relieve this force is for it to bend upward on the high-string side of the instrument. This is the second primary motion of the top! This deformation of the top is minor when compared to the deformation caused by the bridge foot on the bass bar. However, it is definitely important.

When you release the string the top returns to its normal original configuration. If the top just did this once, it would be called a flutter. But the string is vibrating, producing a force as it swings wide and then producing no force at all as it swings back to its central position. In doing so, this motion produces the sound. The larger the primary deformation of the top, the louder the note will be. That is why this second and additional motion of the top affects the sound so much.

When I discovered that a wooden endpin could help the sound of the bass at the bottom of the bass, it never occurred to me that the other end of the bass could be improved also. What I didn't realize at the time was that the wooden endpin was more flexible and had less mass than the steel one. This made it easier for the top of the block to bend farther forward toward the center of the bass. This produced a larger primary deformation of the top, which in turn produced a louder sound.

A few years ago I repaired a bass that had a punch hole in the top at the lower end of the bass bar. The wood of the top had broken perpendicular to the grain of the wood. I very carefully put the small shattered pieces back in their former configuration, gluing them in place. I realized that this was not enough to hold them there, so I made an overlay patch that would cover all of them. When I put the top back on, the customer said that the bass had never sounded so loud. Then I realized how what I had done helped the sound. The top was so thin at the end of the bass bar that when the bridge pressed the bass bar down, only the wood at the end of the bar was bending. By strengthening that area I had made the bass bar bend the top for the entire length of the bar, rather than a small piece of the top at the end of the bar. And that is why the bass sounded louder.

Imagine that you drew a line across the bottom end of the top, perpendicular to the center seam and about 6 inches up from the rib at the bottom of the bass. Let us further assume that you reduced the thickness of the top between this line and the rib to 0.08 inch (2 mm). Now, when the endpin block is pulled forward by the pressure of the strings, where do you think the top will bend? It will bend across the 0.08-inch thin part and not across the entire length of the top.

So, even though you can't see the top bending from the compressive force of the neck and endpin blocks when the string is being pulled, that motion of the top is important to the overall sound of the instrument. The reduction of the neck block and the strengthening of the top near the endpin block, as well as using a wooden endpin, vindicates the assumption that the top is bending because of the compressive force of the strings, and that this motion is important to the sound of the bass.

I have seen more than a few basses in which the lower bout was so thin that the end of the bass bar had pulled the top down and in, causing a depression in the top where it should have been round. My repair thickened the top in the bottom bout with a positive impact on the sound. Bass makers, take note.

22 Useful Measurements for Bass

The string spacing at the nut, center to center, should be ⅜ inch (9.5 mm). On a narrow neck, you can space the strings 5⁄16 inch (8 mm).

For a well-dressed fingerboard, the relief on the G-string side should be about ⅛ inch (3 mm) from the underside of the string to the top of the board at the octave. It can be a little deeper for the lower strings, and for arco players it can be a bit deeper overall.

The highest note on the G string at the end of the fingerboard should be a good solid B-flat. C is even better. Judge the length of a new fingerboard accordingly.

The thickness of the combined neck/fingerboard measured at the A note on the G string should be 1½ inches (38 mm). The thickness at the last part of the neck before it starts its curve into the neck butt should be 1¾ inches (44.5 mm). This can vary, plus or minus, by no more than ⅛ inch (3 mm).

On a three-quarter-size bass, the height of the bridge should be about 6¾ inches above the top of the bass.

The thickness at the top of such a bridge should be a scant 7⁄32 inch (6 mm). For a brighter sound, thin down to as little as 3⁄16 inch (4 mm).

The thickness of the feet of the bridge can vary from 1 inch (25.5 mm) to ¾ inch (19 mm). The thinner the bridge feet are, the brighter the sound will be.

The distance on the bridge between the notches for the strings should be between 1⅛ and 1 inch (28.7 and 25.5 mm, respectively) measured from string center to string center. The bridges on most basses have the strings spaced at 1¹⁄₁₆ inches (27 mm).

At the tip end of the fingerboard, the underside of the G string should be a scant ⁷⁄₃₂ inch (6 mm) above the board. For French bowers, the height of the E string should be ⁵⁄₁₆ inch (8 mm). For German bowers, it should be ¹¹⁄₃₂ inch (9 mm). These distances can be reduced by as much as ³⁄₃₂ inch (2.5 mm) for very responsive instruments or players with a light touch.

The diameter of the sound post can vary from ¾ to ⅝ inch (19 and 16 mm, respectively). The thinner the post, the brighter is the sound.

The edge of the post closest to the back edge of the bridge foot should be no more than ¾ inch (19 mm) behind the edge of the bridge foot. Closer will make the sound brighter. Moving it farther away will make the sound darker. Moving the post closer to the F hole will increase the volume of the E and A strings in comparison to the G and D strings. Moving the post closer to the center of the bass will have just the opposite effect. Move the post until all the strings have the same volume of sound. In basses with a weak sounding E string, sometimes moving the foot of the sound post closer to the center of the bass will improve it.

Never use anything but ³⁄₃₂-inch (2.5 mm) flexible wire cable for your tailpiece hanger cable. With the right clamp it is easy to adjust, and it will never stretch, as the newer fabric cord hanger cable will.

The notches for the cable hanger in the saddle should be ⅝ inch (16 mm), center to center. This can be widened or narrowed to accommodate a mode match.

For the tailpiece cable hanger, the minimum distance between where the cable exits the tailpiece and where it crosses the saddle should never be less than 1 inch (25.5 mm). Anything less will impede the ability of the tailpiece to vibrate.

For the E string, the minimum distance from the tailpiece to the bridge should never be less than 7 inches. Anything less will rob the E string of volume.

The correct thickness for rib stock is ³⁄₃₂ inch (2.5 mm).

In flat-back basses, the maximum combined thickness for the back and the sound post crossbar should never exceed ¾ inch (19 mm). Anything more will mute the sound of the bass.

Stand height is the distance measured from the underside of the fingerboard at the neck butt to the top of the bass. It should be 1 inch (25.5 mm), plus or minus ¼ inch (6 mm).

Never lead the ends of the crossbars into the linings. It may prevent them from coming unglued in the future, but it will impede the ability of the back to vibrate properly.

Try to make your neck and endpin blocks as small as possible without impairing their ability to function properly. This will improve the sound of the bass.

Always use wooden endpins. They should always be ⅝ inch (16 mm) in diameter. A thinner pin will break. A thicker one will impede the ability of the endpin to vibrate properly with a consequent loss of sound in the bass.

23 Troubleshooting

In this chapter you will find a list of minor but annoying problems with possible solutions. But be warned: most, but not all, the cures work because the cause you see in front of you may be compounded by a cause that is not so easy to see. You will just have to look further. Be patient and you will succeed.

PROBLEM: The tuning machines are hard to turn. There are three causes for this:

CAUSE NO. 1: The handle or worm gear is bent. The straps holding the worm gear in place may also be bent.

CURE: Try slowly bending the bent metal back into shape. Be careful, and do not try to bend the metal any farther than is absolutely necessary to make the gear functional again. If you go too far, the metal may snap, and then you will have to replace the tuning machine.

CAUSE NO. 2: The bolt holding the wheel onto the spindle is too tight, pressing the wheel against the plate.

CURE: Loosen the bolt slightly, and put one drop of oil between the wheel and the plate.

CAUSE NO. 3: The strings have been lead onto the spindle incorrectly, causing the strings to cross over one another in the tuning box. One or more strings are now jammed up against the side of the tuning box, making turning the machine difficult.

CURE: Lead the strings into the tuning box as recommended in chapter 17.

PROBLEM: One or more strings are breaking in the tuning box. There are two causes for this:

CAUSE NO. 1: The grooves in the nut are not wide enough for the string. The metal winding on the string is catching up against the sides of the groove, preventing the string from sliding any farther. The more you tune up, the more tension you are putting on that part of the string between the nut and the spindle, until eventually it breaks.

CURE: Redo the groove with a wider small rat-tail file.

CAUSE NO. 2: The curve of the groove is lead too steeply into the tuning box and the bottom of the string winding is catching on the bottom edge of the front of the groove.

CURE: Make a new nut and lead the groove gradually into the tuning box.

PROBLEM: One or more strings are buzzing at the nut. There are two causes for this:

CAUSE NO. 1: The groove in the nut has worn down to the point where the string is now actually resting on the fingerboard in front of the nut. Test this by sliding a thin piece of paper under the string up to the nut. If it cannot reach the nut, you have found your problem.

CURE: Place a thin shim under the nut to raise it just enough to raise the string above the fingerboard. Sometimes this doesn't stop the buzz because of . . .

CAUSE NO. 2: Very carefully examine the string in the groove. Bend the string from side to side just in front of the groove. If it moves even slightly in the groove, you have found the cause.

CURE: Take a pencil and draw a mark in the groove that you can see. Now, very carefully start to file down the pencil mark in the groove, starting at the tuning box end of the groove until you reach the front of the groove. Replace the string in the groove and do your sideways bending test again. If the string still moves, repeat the process until there is no movement. This should cure the buzz. If it doesn't, test the string winding to see whether it is loose. If it is, buy a new string. If the buzz still persists, you will have to look elsewhere. Buzzes can be ventriloquists. I once had a buzz that I thought was in the tuning box. It turned out to be the tailpiece hanger cable buzzing inside the hole in the tailpiece, which exited through the end of the tailpiece rather than the underside of the tailpiece.

PROBLEM: The bass is still stiff and hard to play when the sound post is the proper length. There are two causes for this:

CAUSE NO. 1: The strings have been spaced too far apart in the nut. The G and E strings are exerting a lateral force against the lateral vibration of the neck/fingerboard, impeding this natural vibration, with a consequent loss of sound as well as playability.

CURE: Make a new nut making the spacing between the string centers ⅜ inch (9.5 mm) or even a bit less.

CAUSE NO. 2: The static pressure of the bridge on the top is too great.

CURE: This can be alleviated by installing a high saddle.

PROBLEM: A seam has opened up and is causing a buzz.

CAUSE: Seams are the safety valve of the bass. When a bass dries out and loses moisture, it shrinks slightly. The maple back shrinks much more than the spruce top. This pulls the ribs in at the back, creating a tensile pulling force on the top, which can lead to a crack in the top. An open seam relieves this tensile force on the top and saves the top from cracking.

CURE: This is more do not than do. Do not pull the seam together and then hold it there with any kind of tape. When the tape is removed, it will take little flakes of varnish with it and this area will have to be retouched. Do not attempt to glue the seam back together. You will undoubtedly use the wrong glue or use too thick a glue, making subsequent repairs difficult and expensive. Do try to wedge something small between the rib and the plate, to stop the buzz. Use just enough material to stop the buzz until you can get to a repairer.

PROBLEM: The volume on the A string is noticeably less than on the other strings.

CAUSE: Again, the bass has dried out and shrunk bringing the top and back closer together, making the sound post too tight. This symptom is always a sign that the sound post is too tight.

CURE: The best thing to do is to remove the too-tight post and make another the proper length. Save the removed post—it can be reinserted when the bass absorbs moisture and expands again. You can, of course, just shorten the existing post, but this means that you will have to make another longer post when the humidity goes back up. When the post is the correct length, the volume on the A string will return back to normal.

PROBLEM: Notes are buzzing on the fingerboard.

CAUSE: If a lot of notes are buzzing, this means the action is too low.

CURE: Raise the action.

CAUSE: If only one, or just a very few notes, are buzzing, there are two causes.

CURE NO. 1: The first, and most likely, cause is a fingerboard that is either worn or has not been properly dressed in the first place. If you hold a 7-inch straight edge perpendicular to the board and up against the string and slide it back and forth across the offending area with a light behind it, you will probably see a small hill and a small valley. There should be light from one end of the straight edge to the other, showing that the board is slightly but completely curved. See chapter 11. Correcting that should take care of the problem. Sometimes it will not. This means there is another problem.

CURE NO. 2: Take the string completely off the bass. Examine the offending area of the string very carefully under a bright light. You will probably see that the side touching the fingerboard has flattened. This is the cause of the buzz. Turn the string button at the tailpiece around 180 degrees and retune the string with the flat side up. If this does not stop the buzz, buy a new string.

PROBLEM: Loud wolf note.

CAUSE: The note you are playing and having a problem with has excited a resonant frequency of the bass body. The bass body note is only a few hertz in frequency from the played note and it beats against it, causing the wolf note.

CURE: Assuming the sound post is the correct length for the season (the wolf is always much worse with a tight sound post), there is no real cure for this problem, because everything you do to suppress the wolf note also suppresses the volume of the bass. It is an old saying that the better quality of the bass, the louder the wolf. Homer Mensch's Gagliano bass had such a bad wolf on the F sharp on the D string that when the music demanded it, he never played it, leaving that note to the rest of the section. The so-called wolf note suppressors that you attach to a string between the bridge and the tailpiece may damp the wolf slightly, but they also damp every other note on the string to which they are attached. The part of the string between the bridge and the tailpiece must be free to vibrate. If not, all the notes on that string will suffer. I once reduced a wolf note somewhat by pulling the sound post ¼ inch (6 mm) out beyond the edge of the G string foot and closer to the F hole. It is worth a try. But there are no guarantees.

PROBLEM: The entire sound of the bass is still too bright when the sound post is the proper length and positioned as far back from the bridge foot as is safe (¾ inch [19 mm]).

CAUSE: That is the way the bass was constructed.

CURE: Move the bridge closer to the tailpiece by about ¼ inch (6 mm) and move the sound post back the same distance. Placing Teflon pads under the bridge feet can help. You can also lengthen the tailpiece hanger cable somewhat, but do not lengthen it to the point where the distance of the strings between the bridge and the tailpiece is less than 7 inches. This will kill the notes on the E string. You can also try a heavier tailpiece, but this may depress the overall volume of the bass.

PROBLEM: The entire sound of the bass is too dark, despite trying all my setup suggestions.

CAUSE: Again, that is the way the bass was constructed.

CURE: Move the bridge closer to the fingerboard by about ¼ inch (6 mm) and move the sound post forward the same distance. Thin the entire bridge a bit. Replace the ¾-inch (19 mm)-diameter sound post with a ⅝-inch (16 mm)-diameter sound post. Shorten the tailpiece hanger cable somewhat, but make sure that the holes in the tailpiece for the cable are at least 1 inch (25.5 mm) from the edge of the saddle. Replace the tailpiece with a lighter tailpiece. Try the Krazy Glue treatment on the bridge feet.

PROBLEM: The wooden rod endpin is slipping.

CAUSE: There is insufficient pressure on the metal disk separating the set screw from the wood against the wooden rod to hold it in place.

CURE: See chapter 3. Cut a small notch in the wooden rod to hold the disk in place. Or buy a small hose clamp, place it on the rod at the right place, and tighten the clamp. Or better still, get a bicycle seat clamp endpin, per Ron Carter (see chapter 3).

PROBLEM: There is a buzz in the tuning box.

CAUSE: Any number of things may be loose.

CURE: First, check all the little screws holding the tuning machines in place. One or more may be loose. Then, check the bolt holding the gear onto the spindle. It may be loose. Check dangling string ends to see whether they are buzzing against the tuning box. Check the handle on the worm gear to see whether it is loose. Check the worm gear against the metal straps holding it in place. It may be loose.

PROBLEM: The volume of the E string is noticeably less than the other strings.

CAUSE: There are at least five different causes for this. I will list them with their cures in the order in which I would investigate the problem.

CAUSE NO. 1: The sound post has wandered away from its correct position and taken up residency in another part of the bass or is just too tight.

CURE: Reposition the post properly and make sure it is the proper length. The average position for a sound post starts with the edge of the post closest to the bridge foot about ¾ inch (19 mm) behind the bridge foot. The center of the post should be about ¼ inch (6 mm) closer to the F hole than the center of the bridge foot. This is only a starting point. Moving the post closer to the F hole will give more volume to the E string.

CAUSE NO. 2: Check the bridge height. If it is less than 5 inches, there is insufficient static pressure on the top to produce the proper volume on the E string.

CURE: Either put a tapered shim under the fingerboard to raise the angle of the board to accommodate a bridge height of 6¾ inches or reset the neck to a higher angle to for the same bridge height.

CAUSE NO. 3: The bass bar has come loose at the bottom bout end for quite a few inches.

CURE: On plywood basses open the top at the bottom bout just enough to get a hand inside to reglue and clamp the bar. Then, glue a linen patch over the end of the bar. On carved basses, you will have to take the top off to reglue the bar and glue on a linen patch.

CAUSE NO. 4: The neck is off center, pushing the fingerboard toward the G string side of the bass. To accommodate this position of the fingerboard, the bridge has been moved too far to the G string side of the bass, causing a loss of volume on the E string.

CURE NO. 1: Either the neck will have to be reset properly centered or you can try the following: Pull the top of the sound post to the edge of the bridge foot and then push the bottom of the post in about ¼ inch (6 mm) more toward the center of the bass. This may help the sound of the E string.

CURE NO. 2: Make a new bridge by what is called "faking the bridge": Center the bridge feet properly. Then, raise the E string foot until the center of the bridge top is in line with the fingerboard. This means than when you make the bridge, the E-string foot will be longer than the G-string foot. Finish the bridge in this fashion. If you make the edges of the bridge cosmetically proper, the tilt will be hardly noticeable.

CAUSE NO. 5: The string itself is faulty.

CURE: Buy a new string.

There may be a sixth cause. It is improbable, but not impossible: the bass has been so poorly constructed that the top, and/or the bass bar may be too thick.

CURE: Regraduate the offending part(s), using the Carleen Hutchins method (chapter 14).

PROBLEM: You are having trouble getting a top off or a broken neck out of the mortise in the neck block.

CAUSE: The bond was made with too-heavy glue.

CURE: Try soaking with a fifty-fifty mixture of warm water and white vinegar. By doing this you will help break down the glue holding the parts together.

PROBLEM: There is a long crack in the top but the sides of the crack do not line up, one side being about ¹⁄₁₆ inch (2 mm) higher than the other, and now the sides of the crack are jammed up so tightly you can't line the crack up properly to glue it.

CAUSE: The crack was not repaired when it first appeared and now the humidity has swelled the wood up, jamming the sides of the crack tightly together.

CURE: Set a heating pad to low and place it over the crack for a day or two. This will dry out the wood sufficiently so that the crack will open enough to be lined up properly and repaired.

24

My Sound Post Setter

There is an old saying, "Necessity is the mother of invention." My father used to add, ". . . and the father of crime."

When I opened my first shop in 1969, I bought all the tools and supplies I thought I would need. Among them was the standard factory-made sound post setter. It took me only one bass to realize that it was too light to be of much use in moving a post inside a bass. So, I designed one and took my design to the only remaining blacksmith in Manhattan, and he made me something I have been using successfully ever since.

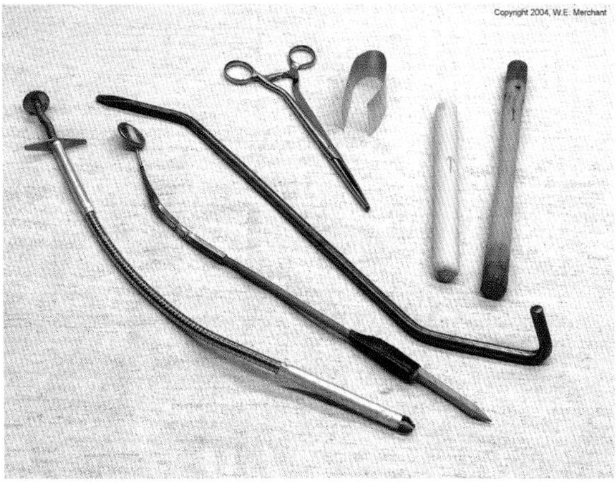

The tools Chuck used to fit a sound post—his custom setter is the middle piece. (Photo by Bill Merchant.)

Over the years more than a few people have commented on how pragmatic my sound post setter is. So, here it is. Take a look at the picture first, and then read this description. The short piece of rod at the end can be bent to the left as shown, or to the right—whatever makes you comfortable. What you see in the photo is the left-handed version. It is made of a metal rod ⅜ inch (9.5 mm) in diameter. It weighs 6 ounces, enough to move a sound post easily with a tap. That is the most important part. The center of the rod is 12 inches long. The two bent ends are 3 inches long.

The setter works effortlessly and efficiently. What more can you ask?

25 Repair Oddments

PUNCH HOLE IN RIB

In chapter 37 of my first book, *The Setup and Repair of the Double Bass for Optimum Sound*, I failed to mention the repair technique for one commonly encountered type of rib damage. This is when a hole has been punched in a rib in such a way as to leave many small pieces of rib scattered all over the place, much like the pieces of a jigsaw puzzle. Assuming that all the pieces are there, this is how I go about repairing this type of damage.

First, I try to find the pieces that fit into the existing part of the rib. Often this is not all the pieces, but you have to start somewhere. I take the first piece and carefully fit it into the rib to determine whether I have the right piece and how well it fits the existing rib. It is very important that this first piece fit as nearly perfectly as possible. If it is the least bit out of line, it will make fitting the subsequent pieces very difficult, if not impossible. Then, I take a very small amount of five-minute epoxy and put it on the edge of the piece to be fitted into the existing rib. It is important to use only enough epoxy to glue the piece in. Any excess will have to be wiped off, with the possibility of destroying the perfection of the fit. This is something you don't want. I then hold the piece in place until the epoxy has hardened.

I continue this process until all the pieces are back together. Care and patience are of the utmost importance in doing this repair. Hopefully you will wind up with a nice-looking repair. If you want, you can reinforce the back side of the rib with pieces of linen or a small cleat or two. Good luck, and go slowly!

CRACK ALONGSIDE THE BASS BAR

In chapter 38 of my first book I covered many types of repair for this crack. I forgot to mention one very important one.

If the crack is right alongside the outer edge of the bar, the best repair for the crack, which will ensure that the top will not sag later on, is to remove the bar. Then, fashion a new bar so that the outer edge of the bar covers the crack by ¼ inch (6 mm). This type of repair may actually improve the sound of the bass.

If the crack is alongside the inner edge of the bass bar, remove the bass bar. Then rout out a small trench in the underside of the top 1 inch (25.5 mm) wide for the length of the crack and centered on the crack to the depth of half the thickness of the top. Then, glue in poplar inlay strips 4 inches long with the grain running at a forty-five-degree angle to the crack, alternating the direction of the grain with each strap. Finish flush to the top and install a new bass bar.

SMALL SPLINTERS MISSING FROM THE EDGE OF A NEWLY REMOVED TOP

Gary Rickman has invented a solution to this type of damage. No matter how carefully and slowly you go in removing a bass's top, there will always be some minor edge damage.

He takes poplar veneer and, using a pressure pad, glues the veneer over the small hole. When the pressure pad is removed, the veneer has sunk into the hole and is glued there. He then sands off the excess. This is one area where it is permissible to sand a part that will be glued later. This is because, when gluing a top back on, you want to make a very weak join, so that if the top has to come off at some time in the future, it is the glue join that will open and not part of the top.

BEFORE REPLACING A TOP

Before removing a top, most good luthiers drill a small hole through the top into the endpin block. Then when they go to replace the top, they take a small, snug fitting dowel and place it through the hole in the top into the hole in the endpin block. This assures them that the top is in exactly the same place at the bottom of the bass as before the top was removed.

You can also drill a small hole through the saddle. Now the entire saddle is the positioning guide. When placing a dowel through the saddle, this is a more accurate guide than a dowel in a hole in the top, which might have some play in it.

FINISHING A FINGERBOARD

Fingerboard blanks ain't what they used to be—straight-grained wood. The grain is often curly and sometimes has small knots. No matter how sharp your plane blade is, it can still dig up small divots of wood (grain runout) when you plane it. Bill Merchant repairs these small holes with Krazy Glue. He fills them with the glue (you can even find it colored black), hardens it with the accelerant, and then sands it flat, finishing with #0000-grade steel wool. Often it takes multiple applications to get it smooth.

26 Bass Thoughts

I have bcen thinking a lot about the bass lately. The more I think that I have discovered all the secrets of the instrument, I am reminded of the history of my discoveries. Every single time I thought I had made my last and final discovery, I learned something new that I had never before considered. So, I have come to the conclusion that although there is a lot of real information in this book, there is still more to be learned, more to be written. I know someone will do it, for the bass is a fascinating and unending source of surprises.

Quite a few years ago I heard of someone who likened the bass to a bow and arrow. He believed that the neck and back were the bow part. The strings were the bow string. The arrow was the bridge and the target was the top. This is not a bad analogy.

I believe the bass is more closely related to a drum. The back and ribs of the bass are the sides and bottom of a drum. The top is the beater head of the drum. And this observation has led me to another discovery. The sides and back of the bass have a great deal to do with the sound quality and the color of the sound of the instrument.

Take the timpani, for instance, rightfully referred to as a kettle drum. The metal tub over which the head is stretched has a definite influence on the sound of that instrument. Consider what would happen to the sound if the metal tub were replaced by a wooden box. Would that drum have the same sound? I doubt it. It would probably sound more like some kind of bass drum.

In the 1950s there was a drummer who made quite a good living by taking the ordinary wooden snare drum and putting fiberglass material on the inside of the drum. This made the snare drum sound even brighter and crisper. And for this instrument this was a definite plus. Many snare drums are made completely of metal to get the same effect (but many drummers prefer wooden snares for their warmer sound).

But let's get back to the bass. What would the bass sound like if the ribs were made of rosewood instead of maple? The sound would have lost its warmth and its depth. It would no longer sound how a bass is supposed to sound.

What follows is pure conjecture. In the early days of musical progress, when the bass was just beginning to take the form in which we know it today, the composers of the time began to hear sounds in their mind that were not accessible on the instruments of the day. And so their luthier contemporaries tried to oblige. They had a general idea of the size of the needed instruments and the necessary type of sound. They began to experiment with various shapes and woods until they reached a general consensus that spruce and maple were the most desirable woods for the sounds they were trying to produce. It was thus that the gamba and violin families began to emerge.

Even today you can occasionally see old Italian instruments with backs and ribs of pear wood. Prescott often used pine for his tops rather than spruce. But over the centuries spruce and maple have prevailed. Why? It is because those woods give the most pleasing sounds that we have come to enjoy and expect from the instruments we are listening to. This type of sound comes from the ribs and back as well as the top.

Not only are the ribs and back vibrating when the bass is being played, but the overtone series produced by the kind of wood used has a definite influence on the type of sound produced.

Here's to the bass. Here's to those crazy musicians who have the courage to play it. Here, especially, is to those researchers and scientists who are trying to make a grand instrument even more magnificent. And, finally, here's to its ever brighter future.

Special Thanks to—

Ron Carter, for his thoughts on sound.

Bill Merchant, marvelous luthier, for his loyalty, his long friendship, his excellent editing of this book, and even more for his thoughtful and highly instructive additions to this book.

Herbert Kramis, world-class bass player living in Zurich, Switzerland, for sending me European products to examine and for his help in dealing with Austrian bass products maker Franz Moser.

Robert Kopec, friend and world-class bass player, for all his help with bass sound experiments on his amazing sounding Christopher bass.

David Brownell, luthier in Ann Arbor, Michigan, for his help in doing a sound experiment.

Bo Stevens, local wood craftsman who makes exquisite marquetry, for his invaluable help in several projects connected with this book.

Ed McCoppin, for his help in obtaining pictures of the smaller instruments of the violin family.

And most of all—Gary Rickman, luthier in Homewood, Illinois, for his innovations and inquisitive mind.

U.S. $19.99 MUSIC/GUIT

STRING INSTRUMENT SETUPS

Of all the knowledge that a good luthier—one who makes stringed musical instruments—can possess, knowledge of proper setup is far and away the most important. Proper setup can change a clunker into a good workman bass. It can transform a very good string instrument into a superb, world-class instrument. *String Instrument Setups: 10 Setups That Will Make Your Instrument Louder, Better, and Easier to Play* is designed to be an encyclopedia of all the latest knowledge on the things that can improve the sound of string instruments.

Chuck Traeger shares his forty years of lutherie knowledge and experience, describing his discoveries in what he calls "Traeger's Principle," the basic principle of how these instruments actually function when they are being played. He provides ten simple setups to individual parts of stringed instruments that will greatly enhance the sound and playability.

Kelly Merchant

CHUCK TRAEGER was born in Manhattan in 1925. He was a successful bass player in New York City, playing in mainstream jazz ensembles. Traeger made his first record in 1945 and continued to record for another ten years. He graduated with a bachelor of science degree in civil engineering from the Columbia School of Engineering in 1959. Traeger opened up his first repair shop in 1969 as a luthier specializing in the bass. He retired from playing the bass at age seventy and has written two other books, *The Setup and Repair of the Double Bass for Optimum Sound* (2003) and *Coda to the Setup and Repair of the Double Bass for Optimum Sound* (2009), both by Henry Strobel, Violin Maker and Publisher. He lived in Yulan, New York.

Front cover design by Tilman Reitzle

HL00160580

8 88680 62374 6

HAL•LEONARD®

www.halleonardbooks.com

ISBN 978-1-4950-6499-9

5199

9 781495 064999